Make Your First Million:
Ditch the 9-5 & Start the Business of Your Dreams

2nd Edition

Martin Webb

CAPSTONE

This edition first published 2009

First published in paperback in 2007 by Capstone Publishing Ltd. (A Wiley Company)

Registered office
Capstone Publishing Ltd. (A Wiley Company), The Atrium, Southern Gate, Chichester, West Sussex, PO19 8SQ, United Kingdom

For details of our global editorial offices, for customer services and for information about how to apply for permission to reuse the copyright material in this book please see our website at www.wiley.com.

Library of Congress Cataloguing-in-Publication Data

Webb, Martin, 1964-
     Make your first million : ditch the 9-5 and start the business of your dreams / by Martin Webb.
        p. cm.
     Includes index.
     ISBN 978-1-906465-54-4 (pbk.)
  1. New business enterprises--Planning.   2. Entrepreneurship.   3. Profit.   I. Title.
     HD62.5.W42 2009
     658.1'1--dc22

                                                                    2009008888

9781906465544

A catalogue record for this book is available from the British Library.

Set in 10/16pt Chianti BT-Roman by SNP Best-set Typesetter Ltd., Hong Kong
Printed in Great Britain by TJ International, Padstow, Cornwall

CONTENTS

INTRODUCTION: WHEN IS A GOOD TIME TO START A BUSINESS?

When is the right time to set up a new business, in good economic times or in a recession? That's a question that I'm being asked more and more at the moment. For at least a couple of years we are all going to be working in a hard marketplace where it is difficult to maintain sales, let alone grow them, and almost impossible to protect your profit margins as competitor companies discount to maintain their businesses and get rid of stock.

My answer to the question is that the state of the economy should not be a major consideration in deciding whether or not to take the plunge, by leaving the comfort of an employer for whom you have worked for some time and going out on your own. This answer surprises some people, but is actually quite logical. As I will show you in detail in this book, you can sum up the key commercial considerations involved in setting up a new business as follows:

- Do you have an idea that will appeal to a market that you can define and then reach?

- Do you feel passionately about that idea and the fact that you can do a better job than the people already serving that market?
- Are you prepared to work extraordinarily hard to get the business started and keep it thriving?
- Have you got or can you get the skills and experience for the actual job you are going to have to do?
- Can you get the funds necessary to start the business up?

In the case of the first four points, whether the country is booming or busting makes no difference to your answer. The last point seems more problematic, with a freeze on credit and the banks licking their wounds, sulking in their tents and refusing to lend money even to people with good ideas. But you can get round that. As we will see in the chapter on getting start-up money, there are other ways of raising finance than impressing a sceptical, and frightened, bank manager of the merits of your idea.

So I think a better question is: What are the advantages and disadvantages of starting the business of your dreams in good times and bad?

SETTING UP IN A TOUGH MARKET

No recession lasts for ever and when the economy picks up you have a huge advantage – you have survived the hard times so the good times should be much easier and very successful. If you start up in a difficult market, you are much more careful about the costs of running your business and buying in the products you need to sell. I have found, through my own and other people's bitter experience, that fear is a great motivator. When you are not sure where the next salary cheque is coming from you grudge every penny the company spends on doing business. This is an excellent way to approach the subject of costs whether you are in a recession or not. In boom times, on the other hand, there can be a tinge of recklessness: everything goes swimmingly and you can get lulled into a false sense of security as your customers borrow and spend. It's easier to remember hubris, the Greek concept that challenging the gods lead to pride coming before a fall, if you have had to struggle for every penny you've made.

Human nature includes some instincts that are not best suited to running a successful business. The fact is that you don't look really hard for cost savings until the fear factor strikes. A law firm I know is a brilliant example of this. Because of the credit crunch its bank lowered its borrowing facility. All the partners and associate partners realized that unless they could find considerable savings to make up for the shortfall they would have to let some people go, always the most reliable way of saving on outgoings. They found those savings because fear made them look harder. For instance, the lawyers were used to paying statutory expenses, such as Land Registry fees, and getting the money back from the client when they put in their final bill, in some cases a considerable time later. By simply getting clients to pay those charges up front they started the process of replacing the bank overdraft not with other forms of borrowings but with savings. And the underlying situation has changed. Where in good times lawyers would have preferred not to ring the client and ask for money up front, they'll do it now because of the fear factor – they'd rather face the wrath of the clients than the thought of redundancy.

Like all managers, those in that firm thought it was being efficient but it was not nearly as efficient as it could be. In all businesses there is much you can do to make savings and a recession makes you do just that – negotiate harder for rate and rent reviews, cancel unnecessary insurances such as for the food in a freezer and so on.

Now look at the opposite side of this hunger for savings, the opportunity side. At a time when everyone is trying to cut costs, along you come with a lean, mean machine of a business able to take on big, unwieldy companies. An experienced recruitment agent got in touch with me and asked if I thought she would be mad to set up on her own when she had just been made redundant by a large company. The large company was suffering in the poor job market when redundancy was more frequent than recruitment. The key to my answer was premises. I thought that if she could operate from her own spare room rather than hiring premises and if she could set up a great website, she could take on the big-boy competitors who are still struggling to pay huge rent and rate bills as overheads in businesses made smaller by recession. She could offer a cheaper service with better terms and conditions than her previous employer at a time when absolutely everyone is looking for savings! In the event she has had to divert to another market, the IT industry, but she is able to find very good people to put up to clients, people who through no fault of their own are on the market. How does she keep up her motivation when business is so hard to come by? She hangs on to the fact that if she can survive this, the good times will be a doddle.

Here's another angle on the argument that the fear factor leads to savings. The worst answer to the question 'Why are we doing business with these people' is 'Because we have been doing so for years and we have a good relationship with their people.' People have a huge degree of inertia caused by their relationships with their current suppliers. There are two lessons here:

1. Don't let it happen to you. Make sure that all your suppliers are aware that you are consistently looking for cheaper ways of buying the products or getting the service.

2. Look for opportunities to shake people out of their inertia by offering better terms. A taxi operator I know offered a perfectly good service from a town about 15 miles away from Heathrow taking business people to the airport. He got an appointment at a big company in the area and offered to undercut its current supplier. The people there were nice but used the 'long time … good relationship …' argument to turn him down. He went back as the credit crunch started to bite and got the business.

So, let's summarize the points that encourage you to set up a business during a recession. It is cheaper to set up: business rents are lower and staff wages are coming down, not going up; there's that fear factor again. Advertising and promotion costs are lower and there is probably less competition. You can even get discounts on your call-answering service and, of course, it's a great time to work hard to lower your bank charges. You concentrate harder on keeping costs down and have the advantage of a lot of potential customers doing the same. In difficult times there is much more flexibility in how you get people to work for you. You do not have to hire them in a full-time capacity or give them a contract that is longer than a few months. You are, as my friend the recruitment agent said, in a buyer's market. Learn fast and negotiate for everything. Be careful, you are not experienced yet and people will take advantage of that if they possibly can. By the way, if suppliers ask you for personal guarantees before offering a line of credit, this is a good time to say, 'No, take it or leave it.' If you do need to rent premises, remember that a landlord can lose the entire profit of a property for a year if it is empty and not earning rent for just two months.

SUGGESTION BOX

Be aware that you are the cheapest resource in the business. You may be drawing a salary, but it will not change if you work eight hours a day, five days a week or sixteen hours a day, seven days a week; nor if you are doing heady planning work or emptying the bins. Be prepared too to do the unsocial hours for which other people would demand overtime. If you can save the money on a cleaner during the first months of the business, learn how to do that job better than any less interested contractor or employee would. The benefits are that your premises look spot on, you've saved a bit of cash and you've learnt a skill that you can supervise extremely well when your business grows and you can get someone in. My motto in the early stages was: 'He who sweeps up cleans up.'

WHAT KIND OF BUSINESS?

There is one big difference in getting going in good times or bad and that is the type of business you go into. Research this carefully. Some things are obvious. A recession's probably not a great time to set up a top-quality restaurant in London where lunch costs £120 a head and the target market is expense account spenders in the City. On the other hand, the financial pages tell me that fast food franchises are doing really well. Sandwich company Subway, for example, is still expanding and taking people on. People are ignoring restaurants but still need to eat when they are tired and have just got home from a hard day's work.

Remember that one person's loss is another's potential gain. As I write, holidays in the Euro zone are hugely expensive for holders of sterling; so everyone is staying in the UK in cottages and other holiday homes – OK not everyone, but you get what I am saying, and people from the Continent are delighted by how cheap it has become to holiday in the UK. Similarly, anyone setting up a business that includes bars are going bust, but they are not the best ones. They tend to be those that have not adapted their offerings to customers or who give poor value for money. I'm not saying that a number of good businesses will not fail as the recession continues over the long term; I'm just saying that if you work out how to run a competitive business well you can succeed.

All of this is not to say that there are not benefits to starting a business when people are spending money freely and finding it easier to borrow. It is easier in a way, but I come back to my first thoughts. The time to go out on your own is when you have a good idea, feel passionately about it, are willing to give it everything you've got in terms of time and hard work, have the skills to do it and can get the seed money to get started. You know you want to do it – so go for it!

PROLOGUE: THE FALSE START

Over the course of eight years, Simon Kirby and I started a business that ran mainly, but not wholly, pubs and clubs. We built up a series of 30 pubs – some of them branded – and sold them for a sum of money that we could only have dreamt about at the start of the project. This book is about how we did it – including the bits we got right and the bits we got wrong. By reading our story you can learn from our lack of business nous and avoid some of the pain and heart-ache that we experienced on the road to entrepreneurial success. The fact that we survived the many ups and downs is a testament to our achievement and gives you the opportunity to learn from the fruits of our labour – from our triumphs and from our setbacks.

It all started with a fairly spectacular failure, a massive blow to our self-esteem as well as our wallets. But we sat down and worked out what we had done so catastrophically badly and this prologue passes on some of what we learnt. It also passes on the change in attitude that the failure brought about; it's not an exaggeration to say that it scarred us for life and strengthened our resolve never to make the same mistakes again.

I was 26. I liked bars and loved music and I thought I would like to own a bar of my own. That seemed the obvious way to create exactly the kind of place I enjoyed going into.

What experience did I bring to bear on the venture? Very little, really. I had earned some pin money as a DJ in nightclubs, but apart from that I had the theoretical knowledge you get from doing a business degree and less than a year's experience as a trainee with the multinational computer company IBM.

I had no experience of running a business, but plenty of experience of drinking and partying. This meant that I had one big asset: I knew the kind of people I wanted the bar to appeal to and I knew what they liked. Simon and I also had enthusiasm, energy and the confidence of youth – vital if you're going to get the world to come along with you and choose your bar to drink in rather than someone else's. Did we have the talents of the entrepreneur at that time? I'm not sure, to be honest, and it's a very interesting question that I'll come back to at various stages in the book.

We raised the cash to get started from a combination of savings, bank loans and maxing out our credit cards. This gave us the £60,000 we needed to buy the lease of an existing bar – the Helsinki – fit it out the way we wanted it to look, buy stock and get into business.

Neither of us had ever refurbished a property in any way, so we did what most people would in the circumstances and hired a building company as the experts to strip out the old and put in the new. We agreed a specification with the builders and a price for a complete refit. They took responsibility for everything; after all, we thought, they must have done this kind of job many, many times. This was, to say the least of it, naïve. More than that, it defied common sense as well as good business practice.

Think of it this way. If you undertake a building project you need expertise, skilled trades people and decent materials. Now, the first time you undertake such a project you may well need to buy in some expertise and employ some skilled trades people. But do you need to pay people to strip the old paper off the walls? And what about the materials – is there something smart you can do in that department? After all, if you put the whole project out to a third party, they buy in materials at a discount and sell them on to you, at least at the full retail price and possibly a bit more. Then they add in another amount for contingencies – the things that they cannot predict as they plan the project – and they'll still charge you that sum even if there are no extra costs. In fact, contractors rarely use the contingency money because when they encounter the unexpected they pass on the extra costs up front – to you! Our contract even included all the furnishings, right down to the tables and the chairs. We got the project done, but we paid through the nose for it and spent much more money than we needed to.

SUGGESTION BOX

Incidentally, if you buy the materials yourself you can probably get a discount too. Try it – ring up your local builders' merchant and tell them you're about to do up your house and that you'll need about £30,000 worth of materials. They'll almost certainly offer you a discount. They may not offer you credit terms, because they only do that when they are sure that they will be paid more or less on time; but it's worth going for that too, you never know. In any case, it's a good exercise for finding out if you've got the boldness to speak to anyone who can help you learn what to do to get your business going.

So, our expensive refit completed, we opened the doors with a triumphant flourish and the party animals of Brighton came flooding in. Within a few weeks we had a packed venue and the cash was rolling into the tills. To say we were cavalier in our approach to spending money is an understatement – we made the Beckhams look like penny-pinchers. Everything was top quality and no expense was spared. There were lots of customers, so we needed plenty of expensive doormen. People didn't want to wait a moment for a drink – well, I didn't at least – so we had loads of staff. We had the top DJs, regular parties both for the customers and also for the staff after work. Best of all, while we knew what all this was costing, we didn't know whether we were making a profit or not; the concept of profit and loss didn't even occur to us. And we didn't have a clue about profit margins either – our strategy was to pitch prices at what people would pay regardless of the cost of the drink to us. The fact was that our bank account was full of money, so we must be getting it right! Then, we started to spend money on ourselves. Our customers were quite well off, you see. They were a wealthy, yuppie crowd and we wanted to share their lifestyle. So we bought fast cars, houses we couldn't really afford and got heavily into the gadgets of the day – mobile phones and so on. We were extremely well dressed in expensive clothes.

We were good at using credit to pay for all of this. We didn't pay off the loans, which after all were not due; we put off paying bills for as long as possible and negotiated credit terms up as high as 60 days – this at least we were good at.

After six months of being awash with money, the inevitable happened. The uncomfortable fact is that people will try out any new bar, particularly the trendy ones; bars come into fashion and go out of fashion, and people drift away. The competition hots up too; after all, they've being passing your place and it's heaving with folk who could be spending cash in theirs, so they change their premises and entice people away from you. It doesn't kill you; it just means that, in the long term, you have to live with a lower turnover on average than you had in the first flush of the new business. In our case turnover went down by 15% and, because we had spent the money straight from the till, we were immediately in trouble.

The critical mistake we made here is that we confused turnover – the money coming into the till – with profit – the proportion of turnover that actually belonged to us. We also failed to plan any cover in case of a downturn in business. We were spending money as though turnover would never drop. It's essential to have some buffer of cash in the business, otherwise you're bound to have problems at some point paying your creditors. You also need to have enough financial knowledge and some sort of system that keeps you in close touch with your profitability and cash flow. I'll discuss this in more depth later. Suffice to say that what happened in our business can be summed up by the term 'working capital' – a phrase, to be honest, that doesn't feature much in my day-to-day vocabulary, but it's one that bankers and accountants use frequently so it's best to have a passing knowledge of what it is and then translate that into everyday, practical terms that will help you run your business.

So, if you're not sure what working capital is, you may want to have a look at Item 1 in the Entrepreneur's Toolkit – The General Business Model and Working Capital. You can do that now (and return here to read about the grisly end of the Helsinki) or read it later when you're further into your own plan for building the business of your dreams.

Back at the Helsinki, we hadn't paid the National Insurance Contributions (NIC), we had no provision for VAT and we had fobbed the brewery off about the rent because we could – it was a soft touch – and because we were drawing out all the cash. We'd had a great year and we'd made no provision for the tax bill that would inevitably follow. We hadn't taken any advice and we didn't know there was anything more to running a business than taking money in at the till and then taking it out again to spend.

The chickens came home to roost one night when someone set fire to a pile of rubbish in the doorway of the bar. The fire brigade put it out, but inevitably a lot of water got through to the floor of the pub and we simply did not have the money to repair it. (Self-employed carpenters do understand business, so they don't offer credit to twenty-something bar owners.) The bar started to look a bit shabby and the business started to go down again, this time much further.

The next thing we knew, there was a bailiff coming round to collect a bill for a spirits supplier and after that, the phone started to ring and didn't stop. Every time it rang it was the same story – someone wanted to get their bill paid. Sometimes it was a friendly 'This has probably slipped your mind' and sometimes it was much more serious. Do you know, when my phone rings I still sometimes give an involuntary shudder in memory of those times? I told you the whole experience scarred me for life. It was horrible to go to work and I felt a combination of shame, fear and stress.

So, after less than two years we handed over the keys to an insolvency company and tiptoed away. We were in debt to the tune of £90,000 and we were incredibly fortunate not to end up as a couple of bankrupts. Fortunately for us, we had given no personal guarantees and had the protection of a limited company. It was, nevertheless, a shocking collapse and a massive blow – we had gone from being rich young men about town to being penniless and trying to avoid the very people that we'd been drinking with only a few months previously. (A senior official in the Chinese government under Mao had watched many, many people being hauled off to prison in Mao's frequent purges; but when it happened to him he said, 'It was like an atom bomb landing on top of your head.' I know what he means.)

I've described this period of time graphically because I really want you to know how bad it feels when a company goes down. And remember, I didn't have any dependants; think how much worse it might be if you got your family into financial problems as well as yourself. As I will describe, setting up your own business is a lifestyle choice as well as a career change. You have to think about the risk you are taking in those two different ways; it can be done, but it is a risk and you need to make it as calculated a risk as you can. I'm not trying to put you off, believe me, but the first thing to do when you're going out on your own is to remove the rose-tinted spectacles and look at your situation with the clearest possible vision.

I went back to being a DJ and got a daytime job in a promotions company. I sat down with Simon and we discussed what had gone wrong and what we had learnt. Actually, with hindsight, it was glaringly obvious what had gone wrong.

While we discussed what went wrong, we were already beginning to plan how to start again. People sometimes ask me why on earth, after such a traumatic series of events, we decided to do it over again and I think there are two reasons. One is that, frankly, it never occurred to us not to. We knew how to make a pub successful and we wanted to own our own business and make a lot of money; there was no option, really. I also think we had a determination to prove that we could do it and repair the damage to our feelings and self-esteem: we were determined to get it right this time.

If I sum up the main change in my attitude to running a business arising from the Helsinki, I think I'd say that it has made me quite tight. Don't get me wrong – I still like to spend money, but only when it's earned, the tax has been paid on it and the cash is available. What I mean is that I'm quite tight in terms of monitoring the progress of a business. I hate spending money unless it is really necessary, and if a business is not doing well I tend to look for ways of cutting costs immediately. I continually monitor performance, and when it drops I don't just hope that things will come right in the end, I look for things that we can do to cut costs and increase revenues. I am, by nature, an optimist, but like all entrepreneurs, and salespeople for that matter, I tend to take a gloomy view on business until I'm proved wrong. Maybe there's a hint of paranoia in me, perhaps I do read too much into things, but I'd rather err on that side than ignore the warning signs and just hope for the best.

1

SO YOU WANT TO BE AN ENTREPRENEUR?

You're plainly interested in the topic of entrepreneurship, and I'm going to assume that you're thinking of becoming an entrepreneur and starting up a business. In this chapter you'll get my ideas on:

- What an entrepreneur is
- The real benefits of being an entrepreneur
- The main attributes of an entrepreneur and how to test if you've got them
- The downside of going into business on your own
- The fact that, if you really want to be an entrepreneur, you've got to do something about it now

SO, WHAT IS AN ENTREPRENEUR?

Are entrepreneurs born, not made? To be honest, I've changed my mind on this. I used to think that entrepreneurship's an innate talent and that if you hadn't discovered it and done something about it by the time you left school you probably didn't have it; but now I think that's wrong. Why? Well, mostly because of all the people I've met during the *Risking It All* TV series where a number of people sold up their assets or borrowed money to start premises-based business like pubs and hairdressers. Many of these people have very good entre-preneurial skills, some of them far better than their basic business

1

skills (a fact that can be a bit worrying), and yet many of them didn't make the decision to exploit these skills until they were 35 or older. Somehow we're stifling a lot of entrepreneurial talent, and for us as consumers – who could be getting a better service – and as a country, we're poorer as a result. However, the fact that over two million people a week watched *Risking It All* is a sign that there is a growing interest in people who want to start up their own business.

So, here's my new view: it is most unfortunate that entrepreneurialism is considered, in Britain at least, as being on the edge of respectability. Think about the archetypal entrepreneurs you get in many TV series, like Del Boy in *Only Fools and Horses*, Mike Baldwin in *Coronation Street* and Arthur Daley in *Minder*, and you'll see what I mean. What they have in common is that they are looking for an easy way to make a lot of money and don't really mind how far they stretch the truth or approach the limits of legality to get it.

Now think about the image of real-life entrepreneurs. There's the Richard Branson type. With very little formal education, he's a highly colourful man, full of energy and loads of self-confidence. He's extremely successful in business, building the image of his companies around his terrific ability to attract publicity and come over very well in the media. Now, if that's what it takes to be an entrepreneur, most of us couldn't do it and, because of that, many of us are put off trying. Certainly, many of the people on *Risking It All* were not highly educated – and not shy of publicity, of course – but they couldn't do it the Branson way. What's more, they have perhaps discovered and developed entrepreneurial skills quite late in life.

Take another stereotype – the dour, hard person keeping their underlings in fear, taking tough decisions and basically not caring a hoot if the whole world hates them as long as they are building successful enterprises. People literally tremble with fear when they see

2

that person's car in the car park and know that they're in the office. You can hear it in the way these tough types speak. They use phrases like, 'If you can't identify the problem, then quite simply you are the problem' and 'If you f*** up again, I'm going to get upset.' They don't really want talented people around them who can think for themselves and ignore what the 'dear leader' is telling them to do. Indeed, they tend to fire anyone who gets a bit too pushy or ambitious. (I could name some, but the lawyers would prefer me to assume that you know who I mean.) I just cannot do it that way and neither can many other successful entrepreneurs. This hard-as-nails, hateful dictator is, however, just another popular stereotype that can put us off the entrepreneurial species and make us feel that we can't do it ourselves.

In fact, there is no model for an entrepreneur: we come in all shapes and sizes and, although we have some traits in common, how we go about building our businesses depends on our individual personality, education and, most importantly, the way we relate to people.

In some ways it's a pity that Branson's lack of formal education is such a highly touted fact (however true or false it is), because, again in my experience, education is a great thing for entrepreneurs, as well as everyone else. As you'll see, I believe in getting as much knowledge and experience of business as you possibly can before you jump off the high board of your first enterprise.

Come to think of it, there's another reason why so many people come to entrepreneurship late. I think the education system itself is partly to blame. Schools have little if anything to do with entrepreneurship training. There are no exams in being an entrepreneur, because there are no courses in it. Unlike becoming a solicitor or an accountant, there is no career path for the entrepreneur, so the careers teachers don't have it on their list. There's just no reference at school to being the boss of your own business. So we're not encouraged to become entrepreneurs at school and in many cases we're discouraged by teachers – 'Oh, it's a terrible risk, don't touch it, you'll probably fail, you'll never have a pension and you'll end up a hard and nasty person.' Attitudes like that can sap your energy and your confidence and, as we will see, you need the opposite of that: you need a very high level of confidence to make a new business work. All in all, I think most of us are conditioned by the time we leave school to believe that we can't actually get out there, start up a business and be a successful entrepreneur.

So we need to add entrepreneurship to the curriculum in schools and universities. Incidentally, there is some movement in this direction within the education system: at Brighton University there are entrepreneur workshops, which is, at least, a sign of progress (so I'll get off my soap box now).

Mind you, there's plenty of good advice around too. If you're thinking of becoming an entrepreneur, it can be extremely useful to go and get a bit of experience in a big company, before you think about the great leap of setting up your own business. You can learn a lot by working in an established business, and it needn't take a long time. In fact, you should see getting some experience as part of the educational process of becoming an entrepreneur and I would advise you to do it. For instance, even four or five months working in a restaurant kitchen will help you take a massive step forward in learning about logistics, the key health and safety rules and so on.

Try to spend time with more than one company and choose ones that you respect. If you're going to open a coffee shop, get a serving job at Starbucks. You may not like the mega-chain if you're going to set up an individual specialized shop yourself, but you can learn loads from Starbucks' years of experience. Basically, the company's paying you to train for the time when you start up your own business. One of the many surprises I've had when talking to new entrepreneurs is that they're happy to jump into a new industry without finding out much about it. A bit of experience is absolutely crucial. In fact, it could be your first step towards setting up the business of your dreams: take a weekend job in any role at all in the sort of business you're interested in starting; you'll learn buckets – yes, even at McDonald's. And there's a second advantage to that plan. Weekends are the times when you spend money that you don't have to spend, on shopping and partying, for instance, so the evening and weekend job gets you to save money and live frugally, a very good habit to get into before you go it alone.

SUGGESTION BOX

You not only need experience in working in the type of business you're going to set up, you also need knowledge of what it's like to be an entrepreneur. Get into the habit of speaking to the people who run the businesses that you go into as a matter of course. Ask them how their business is going; most people are delighted to talk about their own business, and answer questions about how they set it up and what they've learnt along the way.

The strange paradox is this: in one important way, the best time to set up a business is when you are young and don't have any dependants. The risk of wrecking your life, or other people's lives, is at its lowest at that point. If you leave it until you're in your mid-30s, you're going out on your own when you've got a mortgage and probably a partner. There will only be one income for a few years when the kids come along and this all adds to the lifestyle risk of starting a business;

and when it's a bigger risk, guess what? It's easier to say no. The fear factor is the biggest stopper of budding entrepreneurs and in many cases that's quite right too. You should be scared, because it's a big risk.

I think there's another reason many people lack the confidence to have a go, and that's the fact that some of us are rather reluctant to say that one of the biggest motivations for starting up in business is to make money. Most entrepreneurs are passionate about their businesses – they really feel that they are going to make a difference – but if you scratch the surface of this passion, they also want to make money. I discovered this on several occasions in the *Risking It All series*. A lot of couples expressed their dream of offering a service second to none, a step forward in the public's awareness of the way ahead in eating or hairdressing experiences and so on, but all of them eventually admit that money is a huge motivator. And why not? If it were not for the money motivation, we wouldn't have half the innovative ideas that make modern life just that bit easier and more enjoyable.

I don't want to put anyone off starting up a business, but I know some people are not going to like what I'm about to say. For some people setting out on their own is a dream that will always remain just that – a dream. 'It's better to travel than to arrive,' is their slogan. You know that one of Bart Simpson's catchphrases is 'I'll do it in the afternoon.' Well, the catchphrase of the entrepreneurial dreamer is 'I'll do it next year.' They tell everyone that they are seriously thinking about starting a business. They can accept the fact that their career has stalled this year by promising themselves a new one in their own business next year. Next year is always so comfortably in the future that it lets you off the hook of doing anything now. And that's why most people never achieve their dreams.

I believe in the catchphrase 'I'll do it now.' Here's how it works. Everyone who is thinking about setting up a business is going to face a lot of problems, obstacles and barriers: fact. If you don't start dealing with these barriers, you're never going to get off the ground. 'So,' say the dreamers, 'I've got a brilliant idea and I would go on my own if I had the money, and the kids had finished school, and we hadn't just moved into a new house, and we didn't need a new stair carpet and the cat hadn't died ...' So this chapter carries a challenge. After you've read it you're going to decide on the first step you need to take to start up your own business and you're going to schedule to do it within the next 24 hours.

WARNING: THINGS TO WATCH OUT FOR

I've learnt not to allow stress in a difficult situation to swamp me and prevent me taking action quickly. I like the expression: 'If you have to eat an elephant, start by eating its tail.' To me it suggests that when you are facing a big problem or a complex project, work out the first thing to be done and get on with it. I am a great user of lists. I have action lists for myself and a note of the activity lists for the key people in the whole business; indeed, all my plans are based on action lists. If you don't dither, you'll probably make progress; even if you do the wrong thing first, being in action will almost certainly help you to know what to do next.

THE REAL BENEFITS OF PRACTICAL ENTREPRENEURSHIP

The first benefit is the immense enjoyment that all entrepreneurs experience through the process of spotting opportunities. It's very exciting to have an idea, make a plan and then carry it through. Making something happen that would never have happened if you had not started the ball rolling and driven it along is exciting and fulfilling. 'I love it when a good plan comes together' was the catchphrase of the A-Team and is not a bad one for explaining the first benefit of being an entrepreneur. (That's the end of the catch-phrases, I promise.)

The next benefit is definitely lifestyle. The owner of a business has to work very hard to make the business a success, but mainly it's quite enjoyable hard work with the ultimate goal of making a lot of money – and that really does keep entrepreneurs going. You're making money out of other people's hard work as well, which is a whole lot nicer than someone making money out of yours. And when you've made the business a success, you have a huge amount of freedom to do what you want. You can take a lump of time off to do the travelling that you've always dreamed of, spend more time with your family or whatever turns you on. After all, there's no one to tell you when to work or what to do.

And then there's the benefit of the business itself. You said you could run a better bar/hairdressers/restaurant/consultancy than anyone else and you've proved it. Your passion for the business has spread to your customers and staff. I enjoy looking at lots of businesses and working out if I could improve on them. If I feel I can, I've got another potential opportunity.

The difference between an entrepreneur and a business manager can be illustrated in many ways, but I think the best illustration is that business managers tend to accept the world as it is, even when the current situation is complete madness. Here's an example. A friend of mine is a business consultant. He works completely on his own and has done for many years. His forte is to go into businesses and get the senior management to go through a process whereby they them-selves produce a strategy for their business. His unique selling proposi-tion is that unlike other consultancies he doesn't pretend to know what that strategy should be; he merely keeps the planning teams to a well-defined process that delivers a strategy that the team has totally bought into.

He got a job with a European electricity supplier of the old school. It was a state-owned industry both generating and distributing electricity. The problem was for the two arms, generating and distribution, to come up with a strategic plan that would enable them eventually to be sold off. My mate took his process into the electricity-generating side and helped produce plans for two of the generating stations. It was a big success and the senior managers decided they wanted to expand the process into the rest of the 30 or so power stations. They asked my friend for a quotation and he put in as high a quote as he thought he could justify – £100,000 – on the reasonable grounds that it made no sense whatever to use a different process for the rest of the stations. The quotation, however, hit a bureaucratic snag: a director could not sign off such a sum without having to go through a complex tendering process devised by the purchasing department. My friend and a major billion-pound-turnover consultancy were invited to bid. Again, my friend put in his top-price quote.

Later in the process, which had absorbed a lot of management time and expense, he got a call from his main contact who was in some distress. 'You'll have to do something about your price.'

My mate was taken aback, thinking that he had overcooked his fee through his certainty that he would get the business. 'Well, I suppose I could have another look at it,' he stumbled.

'Yes,' said the manager, 'couldn't you make it more of a team effort and bring someone else in?'

'But that would make it even more expensive,' said the consultant.

'Exactly,' said his contact, 'Your competitor has come in with a price of £250,000 and if I try to go with your price the purchasing department will laugh at me, saying that it's not possible that a major consultancy had to charge that much when a one-man band could do it for £100,000.'

My mate accepted the challenge, introduced some more people, got close to the competitive price and got the business.

This is straightforward madness. The large company had cost itself a huge amount of money by tendering and then paying much more than it needed to for the service. Why? Because the people dealing with the problem from the electricity side were business managers, not entrepreneurs. An entrepreneurial attitude would never have let this happen. They would never have accepted the tender process in the first place. Somehow they would have got round the purchasing department; but if they'd lost that battle, they would never had got the quotation raised in the way that occurred. On the contrary, they would have got my mate's quote down to a level that he still found satisfactory but was a good bit less than his first bid. The savings to the organization would have been in the region of £40,000 for the cost of the tendering exercise and the lower price. And things like this happen in large organizations every day. Here is the practical benefit of the entrepreneurial spirit: internal entrepreneurs would have relished taking on the purchasing department and winning, and they would have felt a sense of accomplishment when they got the final bid down by, say, 10%. The business manager, on the other hand, was under stress and being bullied by the purchasing department. He had neither the motivation nor the confidence to change the way the world was working.

Here's another angle on the same thing. A man who had risen to the top of a FTSE 100 company was asked the secret of his success. It's interesting to note that he replied that he didn't know, but that he had noticed that when he moved on in the organization, the job he had been doing was always abolished. This means that he never accepted the status quo. He changed the organization to meet its real needs as opposed to the out-of-date picture of the needs of years ago. The reason everything was out of kilter is that non-entrepreneurs had simply accepted how things were and had tried to change nothing.

So, if you're in a large organization right now, look around and see this type of bureaucratic nonsense and political infighting. If it makes you feel that you'd rather be in an organization that is run for the maximum benefit of the customers, the staff and the owners, then you understand the benefit of being your own person.

Lots of people want to start their own business because they hate the job they're in and can't stand the thought of still being there until they get their gold watch. That's not a bad reason, but it's a negative reason. It's more likely that you will succeed if, as well as wanting to move on, you appreciate the benefits of enjoying the challenge of new opportunities and taking risks. If you want to make a difference, there's no better way than doing it yourself.

SUGGESTION BOX

You can get a bit of practice at being an entrepreneur instead of a business manager by taking on the organization at any point where what is happening is actually damaging performance. For example, if you are running your own profit and loss account or budget, and are limited to buying a service from an internal department at prices determined centrally, challenge this. If you know that you could get a better service from an IT source different from your own in-house department, get a quotation and then make a fuss with your boss and the IT department. Aim either to go outside for the service or to get the internal price reduced. After all, you'll make a better return on the increase in your budget than any IT department over-reliant on its captive customer base and getting fat on that.

THE MAIN ATTRIBUTES OF AN ENTREPRENEUR

A sure sign that you are a potential entrepreneur is shown in your attitude to businesses that you have dealings with, either as a customer or through your working life. I get really restless when I see something being done badly or even not as well as it could be. Perhaps you go in to have your hair cut and simply become aware of the fact that the whole experience could be much better. Perhaps you notice the unsavoury sight of cut hair lying unswept on the floor, or you are ignored by the person at reception even when the time for your appointment has passed. Perhaps your observations have a more positive slant. You feel that although there are grooming products and cosmetics on the shelves, no one ever asks you if you want to talk about them or explains their benefits or suggests you might like to buy them. Perhaps it's the strategy and objectives in this hairdressing business that seem wrong – why are there still only two stylists when there have been four workstations for all the years you've been coming in? If, like me, you think frequently that you could do better than the people you're dealing with, then you've got one vital attribute of the entrepreneur at least. Don't be held back by feeling that it's not your place to get on and turn your observations into business reality.

There's a lot of selling to do. Entrepreneurs spend a lot of time persuading people to do things that they wouldn't otherwise do. Apart from your customers, you're also selling to your bankers so that they come up with whatever facilities you think you need. This is always harder when there's a recession on. You're selling to your suppliers as well – why should they give you better discounts, what's in it for them if you do a joint promotion, why should they lend you money to expand your business and give you 60 days to pay your bills? In a way you're selling to your staff too. You want them to do the job in a certain way, and you have to show what's in it for them if they do.

In fact, I've always found a close relationship between the attitude, skills and activities of salespeople and entrepreneurs. Now, you may not have much experience with entrepreneurs, but all of you will have spent time talking to and being sold to by salespeople. You know the stereotype: 'What do you do when you've shaken hands with a salesperson? Count your fingers.' From our experiences with poor salespeople many of us will take a sceptical attitude towards all of them. This puts up a barrier that the salesperson has to overcome if they are to make progress.

Indeed, many organizations fear their own salespeople. They seem to be young for the money they can make, and often only come to the attention of the rest of the company if something has gone wrong and, for example, a company is spending time and money trying to deliver a salesperson's promises. We need to remove this fear and replace it with a wary respect for the salespeople doing the front-line job, whether it's a waiter in a restaurant or a person involved in selling catering services to large organizations. There is a cultural point here, with the USA having gone further down the line in this regard than Europe; indeed, my comparison with salespeople and entrepreneurs is borne out by this phenomenon – Americans love entrepreneurs and salespeople, while Europeans are still massively suspicious.

So, what can we entrepreneurs learn from the job of selling? Well, salespeople can be divided into 'hunters' and 'farmers'. Hunting is about bringing in new customers, whereas farming is about increasing the amount and type of business you do with your existing customers.

For hunters, the main requirements for success are persistence and the ability to take knocks. Their job demands that they make approaches – by telephone or in person – to complete strangers who may be unaware of the benefits on offer and who are frequently antagonistic to such unsolicited contact. You'll certainly experience some of this hostility when you're out on the street trying to interest people in your new enterprise.

Hunters generally work quickly and have short attention spans. They will usually feel very dissatisfied if any complications arise – whether with the product they are selling, or with decision-making processes somewhere along the line – that interfere with the closure of a sale. They are opportunists, and in most cases will need some kind of monitoring to make sure that the product they are selling is suitable for the purpose and fulfils the promises stated in their sales talk.

Some would say that it is the hunters who give salespeople a bad name and there is some truth in that. But the flip side is that they are also the people who make innovation possible and en masse bear a lot of responsibility for driving the dollar round in a growth economy.

The hunter is the salesperson who gets a high level of job satisfaction in receiving a first order from a new customer. A seller of reprographics expressed it in this way:

'You actually have to start by getting yourself invited into the buyer's office. Then you must convince a probable sceptic that what you are offering has benefits over continuing with the people he or she has previously done business with, perhaps for many years.

'Then you have to find a project, bid for it and win it. The great feeling is that you made it happen, and if you hadn't made the first move and then followed through, then that company would have remained loyal to its existing suppliers.'

The typical conversation of a hunter might go like this: 'I thought I'd do one more door' or 'I stitched him up in no time flat.' If you've worked alongside these people, you're likely to recall other phrases and sayings that you've overheard in coffee breaks and so on.

Many people find the prospect of doing the hunting job horrendous, but entrepreneurs who recognize the dependence of business on such people are themselves continuously selling, and encouraging their people to do the same.

Farmers, on the other hand, develop different but complementary skills to the hunter. They forge long-term relationships and build deep knowledge of their customers. A professional sales team selling computers, for example, might build such an extensive database of customer knowledge over the years that the customers themselves may envy it! The benefits to a company of professional farmers comes in terms of predictable orders, competitive intelligence, market changes and much more. Once again, the lesson for the entrepreneur is obvious. These salespeople study their customers and keep studying them as habits and desires change over the years.

Farmers need to know the results of market research and, of course, of actual sales. The more they know about how their market operates, the more able they are to make innovative proposals and achieve expanding sales targets. Every salesperson, however, has to have some of the hunter attributes. A good farmer who hates or claims to be bad at new business selling may be too slow to go for the order or not sufficiently assertive to win against the competition.

Now let's jump from the salesperson to the entrepreneur. As an entrepreneur there is a crucial balance of activity between hustling to get things done and farming for the long term. Observe closely the salespeople you will talk to as you set up your business: you can learn a lot from them, in terms of how not to do it as well as how to do it. So being a good salesperson is one attribute of the entrepreneur. What else is there?

HAVE YOU GOT WHAT IT TAKES?

As an entrepreneur you will need to be self-critical and a good listener, even when you're listening to bad news. You have to be able to evaluate feedback and act on activities that you need to change. You also need to be self-confident so that you can survive the knocks and persevere.

For example, we were turned down for a licensing application for a particular club, but had to persevere to keep on the plan. We had to be prepared to lobby the right councillors, reinstate the application and reapply. In the end, we not only got the licence but recovered the costs of the original application as well.

You need the sort of self-belief that makes you certain, not fairly sure, that you will do the job better than anyone else. In decision making, for example, I know that you're weighing up options and there is uncertainty in your mind about what you're going to do, but once you've made the decision, go for it like a demon, or an entrepreneur, possessed.

So how do you work out if you've got what it takes? 'Know thyself' was the motto above the oracle at Delphi and it's good advice. From the attributes people have discussed with me as important, and from my own experience, I have put together this simple self-assessment scheme to give a clear indication of whether or not you are a suitable case for joining the ranks of the small businessperson or entrepreneur. How well do the following attributes describe you?

Fill in as follows:

Answer the questions with: **1** Yes; **2** Mainly; **3** Not really; **4** No

I am a good listener:	**1 2 3 4**
I hate putting things off:	**1 2 3 4**
I tackle hard jobs before easy ones:	**1 2 3 4**
The family supports my decision to set up on my own:	**1 2 3 4**
I am ready to work all day, every day when necessary:	**1 2 3 4**
I have good self discipline:	**1 2 3 4**
I can sell:	**1 2 3 4**
I like selling:	**1 2 3 4**
I take calculated decisions confidently:	**1 2 3 4**
I deal well with stress:	**1 2 3 4**
I learn from my mistakes. I don't dwell on them and I don't let them knock my confidence:	**1 2 3 4**
I believe, in fact I'm certain I can go it alone:	**1 2 3 4**
I can motivate people:	**1 2 3 4**
I can think long term:	**1 2 3 4**
I can visualize how things will be when I am successful:	**1 2 3 4**
I finish activities even when I've had to overcome lots of knocks:	**1 2 3 4**
I can do without the trappings of big companies – For example kick off meetings, award ceremonies, company sponsorship and parties:	**1 2 3 4**
I like to be in control:	**1 2 3 4**
I prefer to work to a vision or an objective rather than just carry out tasks:	**1 2 3 4**
I understand the risks of going on my own:	**1 2 3 4**

Analysis – add up your score by totalling the numbers in the boxes you have marked.

- Score 70–80: You are not by your own estimation the type to go plunging in to a small entrepreneurial business.

- Score 50–70: Hmm. You have some of the traits of a plunger-in at the deep end, but have another look at the areas where you scored 3 or 4 and ask yourself if you could improve with practice. If the answer to that is yes, then have a go by all means but be prepared for a few sleepless nights.
- Score 30–50: Go on, go for it. You don't enjoy the big company that much, so think of the benefits of being an entrepreneur.
- Score 20–30: What are you waiting for, stupid? You are a natural. You should have done it years ago, so come on in, the water's terrifying.

Hang on, you have only done the easy part of 'Know thyself'. Now ask your nearest and dearest and then some trustworthy colleagues to agree or disagree with your own assessment.

I can't leave the topic of the attributes of an entrepreneur without emphasizing a point that feels like stating the bleeding obvious – use your common sense. When I look at some of the decisions that business people make, I'm sorry, but some of them are just plain stupid. I can't believe that anyone could have an expensive mid-town café premises with a passing trade of office workers going to work from 7.30 am, and not open it up until 10.00 am. But I've seen it done, cleverly, or stupidly, losing lucrative breakfast sales in premises that are already paid for. So much of entrepreneurship comes down to using your common sense.

Will it make a million?

Look, let's be realistic. If your ambition is to buy a village post office, go through the training to become a postmaster or mistress and run the shop yourself, you're not going to make a million. It still may be a good idea, and it may give you the lifestyle you're looking for, but it is not a huge money-spinner that you can sell to the likes of Wal-Mart for the thick edge of a billion pounds.

An idea that's going to make you a million is a bit different and, if that is your goal, you need to check out in the first place whether the idea is likely to really fly. The technical term is expandability. One retail outlet is unlikely to make you a million, so you need an idea that will expand into other outlets or, for example, into a franchise.

Think again of the hunter/farmer analogy. The hunter part of you is going to be dedicated to getting the business started and managing the first outlet. The farmer side of you is thinking ahead to what can happen once the first business is a success, and even as far as the exit strategy – how are you going to cash in? Who or what type of company are you going to sell the business to? How many outlets will you need to make an interesting proposition for another entrepreneur to buy into? You don't need to have a lot of detail at this time but it needs to be in the back of your mind – the objective is the first million!

Take the first step

OK, it's time to get down to brass tacks. You've got a good business idea that you think could beat its competitors if it was implemented in the way you envisage. That's a great start. Now make a list of what you would have to do in order to get this business started. Include problems like having no money, but put the problems down as challenges rather than problems – don't write 'I haven't got the money', write 'I would have to raise a substantial sum of money to get started'. The list will be long:

- I've got to find premises
- I've got to find and negotiate with suppliers

- I need a business plan
- I've got to refurbish the premises
- I've got to learn about VAT and other administrative issues
- I've got to get the family on side
- And so on …

Now ask yourself what the first step is that you could take immediately to start the ball rolling. By all means identify more than one thing that you could start now, but make absolutely certain that you have recognized the first step. When you have finished your list and decided on this first step, do it now, before you read on. If that isn't possible, like if you're on a train, then schedule when in the next 24 hours you're going to do it; because in my experience, if you can't find time to start the first step in the next 24 hours you don't really want to do it at all. By the way, why haven't you done it already?

A mate of mine was thinking about moving out of a house he and his family had lived in for 14 years. You can imagine what had gathered in his attic after bringing up a couple of kids during those years. It was an absolute nightmare that he solved by doing 20 minutes every day tidying, throwing out and making the problem manageable. There's a lesson there – start early on a difficult task and don't try and do it in one huge blitz.

When you are an entrepreneur. lots of people come up to you and tell you about their dream for starting a business. Some of them are really wild and you get the idea that they're dreamers, so I use the first-step challenge as a simple test of their real intentions. The first time I used it was with a man I knew who kept talking to me about his ideas for going on his own. He was going to start a copying shop, or a laundrette or whatever. He always had a good reason why the idea was better than its competitors at the time and I honestly thought that he was going to make the decision at some point and do it. Then he came to me with his latest idea – making kayaks in his garage. He had found an overseas supplier who supplied kayaks in kit form. It was quite tricky, but my pal had good do-it-yourself skills and was confident that he could supply a good product and certainly a much better product than an individual without his skills. I remembered that his garage was, like most garages, completely full of the flotsam and jetsam of normal life and you could hardly get into it, let alone build a kayak in it. So I suggested that he should immediately take the first step and clear the garage that weekend. The garage is still chockablock and that was ten years ago; but there's no harm in dreaming, unless you want to have fun and make money. To do that, you have to move on to Chapter 3.

This book starts with the story of C-Side. It describes my experience in setting up and selling that business over a period of ten years. I will share what I learnt that worked and, just as importantly, what I learnt not to do. I'll also illustrate my points with stories from the experiences of the *Risking It All* contributors and other entrepreneurs that I've worked with.

Then we move on to The Entrepreneur's Toolkit. It's a collection of the theories and processes needed to run a business properly. I've put links to the toolkit in the early chapters. For example, the C-Side story includes my fascination with cash flow, so there are cross-references to items in the toolkit that show you how to create and keep company cash flow up to date. You may choose to read it while you're still reading the first seven chapters or come to it in due course as you go through the whole book. The toolkit will act as a reference section that you can continue to use as you build the business of your dreams.

PAPER TALK

These are some extracts from articles I've written in the Daily Telegraph. *I've put them in at points in the book that seem to make sense.*

Whatever you do, don't set up a small business. Stop reading this now, pop the kettle on and make a nice cup of tea. Stick to your day job, knuckle down and give up the silly dream of being your own boss. You probably wouldn't like it and who wants to give up a regular salary and the 5 Series anyway?

Still reading? Well, that's the first small test passed. Becoming an entrepreneur requires balls of steel, regardless of gender, and a pumped-up ego that's not going to be easily deflated by the doom-mongering failure merchants who will emerge from among your friends, family and colleagues as soon as you mention you're considering the dash to financial freedom. They do have a point though – just because you think importing and flogging those lovely Balinese beds you saw on holiday last year is going to cover little Jack's school fees and the weekly Waitrose bill doesn't mean that a whole horde of others haven't had exactly the same idea.

2

STARTING AFRESH

Right, you have the germ of a business idea and you're ready to make some decisions on how you're going to set up the new business. In this chapter you'll look at:

- Defining the lifestyle change you're about to make
- The risks of setting up your first business
- Preparing to change lifestyles
- Defining what you're going to sell and to whom you are going to sell it
- Evaluating the feasibility of the idea
- Getting the start-up money

DECIDE WHAT YOU'RE GOING TO DO AND WEIGH UP THE RISKS

Some time ago I got together with three people, each of us put in £5000, and we took on the lease of a derelict licensed bar in the centre of Brighton. Interestingly, and quite by chance, we were starting in a recession. If you begin a business in a recession some people think you're mad, because everyone is tightening their belts and all that; but there are benefits as well. In this case, the landlord couldn't rent the property so we got it premium free – that is, we didn't have to pay an upfront sum for the goodwill of the business. We also got a rent-free period. Next, we employed our youthful enthusiasm and managed to persuade a brewer to lend us £20,000 without any security. We used the money to do the place up. During the next month, the four of us stripped and tiled walls, painted everything and fitted it out in a way that we knew would attract the customer base we were looking for: students (there are lots of those in Brighton) and other young people. We did it all ourselves and were thus able to do a reasonable job at the lowest possible cost. We named it the Squid and Starfish – at the time, a quirky title that set us apart from the competition.

Most businesses need a certain amount of cash to get started and it's very important to put some of your own money in. Doing this is very helpful when it comes to borrowing the rest of the money from banks or whoever: they are highly unimpressed by owners who want them to do the entire funding. So, save and do without for as long as it takes to get together your own start-up finance. We lived as frugally as possible. The natural party animal in us made it quite hard to stop going out, but it had to be done.

There is another benefit to going through this hair-shirt existence. You get used to how you're going to live for the first few years of being in business. We had learnt our lesson from the Helsinki and were determined to take as little money out of the business in the early stages as we possibly could. Ever wondered about who buys the dented tins in the reduced baskets in supermarkets? It's would-be entrepreneurs keeping their costs down to save for their first few businesses. You and your family are going to do without holidays for some time, so it makes sense too to do that before you start. If nothing else, it ensures that the members of your family properly understand the sacrifices they are going to have to make.

This is a good time to talk about the risk you are about to take and its impact on your friends and family. Look at the risk issue in two ways: the risk to your lifestyle and the risk inherent in the business you are going to set up – then ask yourself about the likelihood of success.

Don't delude yourself in any way: be very honest as you think this through. Ask yourself some hard questions. If at the moment you're doing a job that involves managing a team of 25 people with a budget of millions, will you still enjoy owning and working in a restaurant or hairdresser's in two years' time? Or will you be bored stiff? If you know you will be bored, then you must work out an exit strategy at the start to make sure that every decision you take for the business leads towards selling it, putting a manager in, or whatever your plan is for getting out of running the day-to-day operation of the business.

SUGGESTION BOX

You need two visions clearly in your head. The first is the vision of your business – what it will look like to customers, why it is different from the competition and so on. You also need a financial vision. As good as any is to work out what the business will need to be making for you to exit with a million pounds. A rough way to do this – and that's all you need at this stage – is to make a simple calculation of the value of the business to someone interested in buying it. Look at it on the gloomy side as always and assume that a buyer will pay two and a half times last year's annual profits for the business. (This is called the 'multiple' and hugely depends on the industry you're in and the size of your business.) That's quite gloomy because you may do a bit better than that. This means that the profits would have to be one million divided by two and a half, or £400,000. Later on you'll find out from experience how much one outlet can earn in profits and that will tell you how many outlets you will need to get to the magic number.

The next hard question to ask yourself is whether you really have got support from your whole family, or have you just conned them by not explaining the real implications of what you are about to do? Will your kids really be all right about not going on the school skiing trip when the event actually comes round? And will your partner still back you up when a cash-flow crisis means selling their car? In one business I worked with, two couples got together to run their dream hotel. They were best friends, but they needed to think about the fact that the women would get fed up if the men didn't pull their weight with the cleaning and other housework-type chores. Would they still be best friends if one couple felt the other couple were spending too much time away from the business? Once again, use your common sense to work out the potential problems that might crop up with your new lifestyle.

Assess what you're giving up – your home life, possibly your home if that is how you're going to get your starting capital, almost certainly holidays – and that's just what you're sure to go through. If your children are at private schools you are taking a risk with that as well. If the business needs even more money to grow, putting them into a state school would be a considerable saving – but are you prepared to tell the kids that's going to happen? What else? Well, there's your pension and your healthcare plan and the company car that feels as though it's free. You know what's at stake; I just want to make sure you have gone through the list comprehensively. I've come to the view that our business lives are fairly fragile, the line between success and failure very thin, so don't ignore anything that makes you vulnerable – some marriages will not survive when a business goes under.

Now, take the worst-case scenario. What would happen if the business, despite your hard work and enthusiasm, simply didn't fly? Could you and your family cope with downsizing the house, for instance, if that were the only way you get out of personal debt? I'm a great believer in worst-case scenarios. Thinking them through really makes you assess the lifestyle risk properly, or professionally you might say. In the end, if you feel that the worst-case scenario would make you suicidal, then drop the idea and don't jump in.

Right! That's the end of the gloomy stuff and you're still reading, so you must have decided that the lifestyle will suit you and that you could handle the changes if everything doesn't go according to plan. Let's move on and think about the business risk. The biggest risk to any new business is lack of customers. How sure are you that people will warm to your idea as much as you so passionately do? There's only one way to find out – ask them. Speak to representatives of your target market and make sure that if your services were available they would use them. When you're looking for your premises, think about how many of your target market actually walk past on any one day. We'll get to the nitty-gritty of all this when we talk about filling in the forms that banks make you do before they'll lend you money. At the moment you're just looking at the overall strategy and the risk that the business might not work out. Then there's competition – how much is there at the moment and how much might there be later on? It's important to think about the future as well as the present situation – how might the market develop? This is particularly true if technology is involved in what you're offering. Technology changes incredibly quickly: imagine if you stock your brand new Computer Café with technology and within days something comes along that's bigger, brighter, cheaper and two keystrokes faster. It could be a recipe for disaster.

I got my fingers burnt to some degree in a business that bought some leading-edge technology to handle print jobs, except that it couldn't compete with simpler printer technologies on small jobs. So despite the sophistication of the technology, we couldn't make the idea work and I got out of that business. (It's not leading-edge technology, someone has said, it should be called bleeding-edge technology.) As a result of that experience, I tend to go for technology whose teething problems someone else has already solved.

Think about the risk to your costs as well. Projects, particularly building and fitting-out projects, are notorious for going over budget. Make sure you know what you'll do if this happens to you.

It just doesn't make sense to chuck in your job without thinking through what it is you're going to do instead – and how likely it is that your new enterprise will result in a lifestyle that is, at the very least, acceptable to you and your family. I tend to do risk assessment very thoroughly (normally talking – or rather listening – to any expert I can find on any element of my plan) but I do it rather informally. I make sure I've thought about as many things that could go wrong as I can and then make a rather gut-based decision. But entrepreneurs, as I've said, come in all shapes and sizes, so I've created a more formal process, which is Item 2 in the Entrepreneur's Toolkit, Risk Assessment. If it suits you to do so, you can use the process to assess both the lifestyle and the business risk you are thinking about taking.

WHAT IS A GREAT IDEA?

Let's take a reality check here and think about the different kinds of ideas that make the first million. What is a great business idea? I'm going to describe here the attributes of a great idea and also how you might come up with one. I'll use a couple of examples to explain the process of having and evaluating a business idea. Let me try to give an overview, though. A successful business is one that meets customers' needs better than they're met elsewhere. It doesn't have to offer something completely new; it just has to have an element that makes people think 'That's a good idea, I'll try it.'

One of the most common ways of finding your big idea is through the simple observation of everyday life, and listening to people who you come into contact with. One good example of this I came across is of a thirty-something woman with three children. Her experience of motherhood gave her an acute awareness of her children's needs and wants. If the kids saw a toy advertised on television, they wanted it; if they played with a toy round at a friend's house, they wanted it; and they nagged and nagged until they got it. However, once this object of desire was home and unwrapped it would lose its appeal – often in a very short space of time. Our mother-of-three confirmed that this was a common trait by talking to other parents.

Interestingly, the kids wanted special toys at party time, so that their friends could all enjoy something a bit out of the ordinary for the duration of the party; bouncy castles were about the only thing to cover this eventuality. Our thirty-something woman heard other mothers complaining about the price of buying big, expensive toys that they only needed for a one-off occasion.

What's more, although she really liked to give her firstborn new, shiny toys straight from the toyshop, her second and third children were frequently just as happy with the hand-me-downs they got from their elder siblings (not for everything – they liked to have some things that were new to them, but for major items, like a tricycle, hand-me-downs were just fine). She saw that other mothers did exactly the same thing.

Her children often grew out of toys very quickly – the tricycle, so joyously unwrapped, only lasted for six months before it became too small. And she heard similar stories from the women at the school gate.

She understood the frustrations that she and other mothers were facing, and this gave her the germ of an idea – a toy-hire shop that would specialise in larger toys. She would do business from a shop as well as a catalogue and website. She got another mother interested and the two of them started to evaluate the idea.

Another common way of finding your big idea is to take an existing idea that is successful in one culture – a country overseas perhaps – and import it, suitably tailored for the new location.

An example of this is Coffee Republic, a major chain of coffee shops started by the brother-and-sister team of Bobby and Sahar Hashem. Sahar was used to the products and service she could get when she was in New York and missed them when she was in England. In fact, she missed the skinny cappuccinos and fat-free muffins so much that she knew there had to be a market for them. She knew that other people would love them if they were introduced to them – and the rest is the history of Coffee Republic.

Now evaluate your idea strategically by considering the following questions:

• *Why has no one done it before in the geographical location you have in mind?*
  I see many examples of new businesspeople who believe that they can 'create a local market' by changing the habits that local people have built up over years and make them spend their money differently. I get concerned when someone says, 'There's got to be a market for it here; the nearest competitor is miles away.' It makes me ask why no one else has done it there. How can you be the first person to think that this idea will work in this location? Strange as it may seem, I'm more comfortable when there are outlets with a pretty similar idea to yours operating quite nearby. OK, probably

next door is a little close, but if they're miles away then maybe the market is too. Starting a business is struggle enough without having to introduce a totally new concept to a sceptical local market. This was a big consideration for the woman with the toy-hire shop idea – she knew the idea had taken off in New Zealand but there was nothing like it for the market she had in mind – reasonably well-off, professional, middle-class families – in the country, let alone the town where she was thinking of setting it up.

- *Is it expandable?*

  We're not here to get bogged down in running an outlet that's only suitable for a very limited market in a very particular location. The toy-hire shop scored well on this one: the owners even had ideas for franchising the idea as well as opening up more outlets.

- *Have you checked that it's not just you who thinks the need is urgent?*

  Some people have a passion for some very peculiar things. When they try to turn this passion into a business, they find that few people share the passion. Don't get me wrong, I want you to be passionate about the idea and how popular it's likely to be, but don't get carried away. I know you're passionate about taking your new concept to market, and bursting for people to love your products and services as much as you hoped they would. But whatever your motivation for getting into this, it's time to remind yourself about the real motive for going into business – making money. OK, OK, I know you want to have fun doing your own thing; but believe me, there's no fun in running a business that's not making money. As the General Motors Executive so neatly put it: 'We're in the business of making money, not cars.' So, if you enjoyed your holiday in Egypt and got the hang of hubble-bubble pipes and the cafés where you smoked them and drank strong coffee, remind yourself that smoking is in fact banned in public places in the UK! Try not to get into a position where you're trying to push water uphill by choosing an idea that you love but that you're going to have trouble persuading other people to spend their money on. I don't mean to suggest that you should ignore intuition and passion. What I'm saying is that you should tune your intuition to think not about innovation in product terms or in terms of a new market, but about the link between the product and the market. Keep asking yourself, 'What is my strategy? What am I trying to sell and to whom am I trying to sell it?'

PAPER TALK

The secret, in my experience, is to listen patiently to everyone who wants to tell you why your new business idea is rubbish. Fix a Blairite grin to your face and thank them for their opinion. Then run crying to your secret place and work out in private whether they've thought of something you've missed. Crucially, you've got to ask yourself why a particular individual has offered their opinion in the first place – there's more politics to this than a presidential election campaign. Current workmates will be envious of your upstart ideas and may damn them with faint praise; close family will worry you're consigning them to Lidl and travelcards for the foreseeable future; friends will tell you what you want to hear; and parents will wonder if the money they spent on your education is going to be wasted after all. Funnily enough, it's often complete strangers who will offer the healthiest advice, like the bloke in the pub whose mate had the same idea, or the mini-cab driver whose insightful comment convinces you he's a moonlighting Harvard professor studying the start-up turmoils of British entrepreneurs.

There's normally at least a grain of truth in most advice that will be dished up in your direction. The key is to pick those grains from the sludge of distain, jealously, *Schadenfreude*, envy, worry or fear that will inevitably surround them. Once you've done that, you can start to see if your original idea still stacks up and is as viable as you first thought. Take your time over this. Changing your mind at this stage and admitting your idea was weaker than a homoeopathic hangover cure will cause you some mild irritation (as the 'I told you so' looks and comments are dispatched your way), but at least you'll still have a roof over your head and a credit rating. Plus you won't have failed. But you won't have succeeded either.

IDENTIFYING YOUR PRODUCT AND YOUR MARKET AND FINDING THE START-UP MONEY TO ATTACK IT

Right, let's talk about markets and marketing. To be successful you have got to get right inside the heads of your customers so that you know not only what they need and want now, but also what they're going to need and want next year. To be honest, this was relatively easy for us at this stage of setting up C-Side, because we were already close to the people we wanted to attract – they were our friends and our peer group. We were young, trendy people in our mid-20s. We were into music, pubs, clubs and going out. Our customers were all of these things too; we knew them inside out because we *were* them. Having got to know this market we never lost sight of it and, as the story unfolds, you'll see that we concentrated on the same people for the whole time of C-Side, selling them different products and keeping up to date with their feelings and aspirations, despite the fact that we grew out of that age range and changed our priorities.

So, back to your developing plan. Describe and perhaps write down a detailed description of the type of customer you are going to appeal to with your new business. What is their background, what do they do, what papers do they read and so on? Get out there and talk to them not only about your idea but also about their general aspirations and desires. Read the magazines they read and look at the adverts in them – they're a good clue to how marketing people think businesses should address this market.

Think of it this way. There is no such thing as a product without a market, just as there is no such thing as a market if you do not have a product for it. So, think in terms of 'product markets'.

When you have been on your own for a while, you will be surprised by how many other people are thinking of doing the same as you: leaving the big company and going out on their own. They will speak to you about their ideas and ask for your comments. Usually they take what I believe is the wrong approach. They have, for example, thought of, or developed, a new 'product'. It's an innovative idea for, let's say, selling educational aids – a package of training aids and books that they used to teach themselves how to appreciate grand opera, a 'starter pack' for someone who wants to enjoy opera but hasn't a clue about where to begin to study and learn about it. They have computerized the product and think that with a bit of investment and work it could become marketable. And they could be right.

Unfortunately, though, what they have is a product, not a product market. They do not have a product market until they have a customer. So, here's my advice: the moment you have the thought of a product, identify the market for it and think in terms of the product/market.

There's another way of doing this: start with the market. Look at a market or group of people that you know and understand. Perhaps it's the managers and people you have been dealing with for years in a big company. Think of their passions, hobbies and general needs and wants at work and at play. After all, you know them well, so you know their gripes and grievances as well as their wants and aspirations. Now, think of a product or service that they might buy. If you can, think of another one and another one until you have generated a list of a series of products to meet the demands of this market.

Another example of this process of creating lists comes from my experience with C-Side. Even a single bar in, say, a town centre can cater to more than one market and sell them different products.

The first market is lunchtime office workers and corporate hospitality; the second is evening office workers before they go home. At night your third market arrives: customers coming out for a meal or for a drink after they've eaten. Then there's Saturday lunch, and so on. You may have to vary your product and services for each of these markets. You may have to have different menus, different music, even a rearrangement of the furniture to meet the particular needs of the product/markets you are serving.

To be honest, I don't really like trying to make a pub too different at different times. You can fool yourself into thinking that you can attract a different set in the evenings; but don't forget that your décor stays the same, as does the presentation of your products. Never let your common sense be overcome by any sort of wishful thinking. However, I'm including this idea because it may help with the kind of business you're planning.

WARNING: THINGS TO WATCH OUT FOR

If you're going to understand your customers, you've got to be continuously in touch with them. I learnt that I couldn't do that if I was actually behind the bar. This made me avoid serving at all costs, using staff instead. I know that you may have to start by serving the customers yourself, but get out of it as quickly as you can. Remember the objective: one million pounds. You've got to learn how your customers will develop their needs and wants in the future and translate that into tuning the products and services you offer. And, of course, you need time away from the business or you've already started to look for the next premises or work out how you can make more money from the current one. Some entrepreneurs actually want to do the direct selling to customers in the premises and that's fine; but it's a much harder way to make a million.

Right, let's recap for a moment. You've started to save money to put into the new business; you've got a vision of the lifestyle that you would prefer to the one you have now; and you've assessed the implications of things not going well and decided to take the risk. You've thought about the position your business will have in the market and what will distinguish it from its competitors, now and in the future. You have a clear idea of the market you're going to address and done some overall research on it. It's time to find the premises for the business – but just before that, it's time to think about money and where the start-up money is going to come from. You'll find some ideas for sources of money and how to get to them in Getting the Start-up Money – Item 3 in the Entrepreneur's Toolkit.

PUTTING THE IDEA INTO PRACTICE

Right, you've got the great idea, you know roughly where you're going to get the start-up money, you've got everybody necessary on board and it's time to get started on the outline planning of the business. In this chapter I'll cover:

- Checking that you actually need premises in the first place
- What you have to do to find the best premises possible for the new enterprise
- Drawing up the first rough financial plan
- The considerations you have to take if you have a choice between buying and leasing
- When and how to review your strategy if the business doesn't start off as well as you hoped

DO YOU ACTUALLY NEED PREMISES?

I think it's difficult when you're chasing the dream of running your own business to remain dispassionate at the same time as pursuing passionately what you want to do. It's almost a paradox. Nowhere is this more apparent than when you consider the emotional topic of getting premises from which to run your business. It is exciting to plan how the place will look, what the signs will say and what the look and feel of your 'business baby' will be. But think about it. Whether your idea is a fresh look at an old product or a complete innovation that you have to attract the market towards, you're adding risk and danger if you go into your own premises straight away. Use your hard-boiled business head to weigh up the pros and cons.

Leasing premises to experiment with a new business idea adds risk to the venture because you have to use a hefty lump of cash to fund it right at the start of the project. If, of course, you're going to run a pub or a restaurant then there is no alternative – you've got to find a location for the business. But ask yourself if it's really necessary to saddle yourself with such costs if you're going into a venture that could take other routes to market.

Suppose, for example, your thing is art and what you want to do is to sell modern paintings. Perhaps the instinctive decision is to go for an art gallery, stock it up with the sort of paintings you're introducing to the world and take it from there. The chances are high, of course, that you will also design and build a website and that you may in the future go through the process of making it possible to buy art directly from your website. Maybe that's your second phase.

But think of the costs of going straight into having premises. You've got to lease the place for at least half a year, probably more. That's anything from £1000 to £4000 a month for starters. Doing it up could easily cost £10,000 as an absolute minimum. You'll need staff cover in the shop when you're away evaluating and buying stock, and there are utilities, insurances and so on to consider too. It's a big sum out of your original investment at a time when you can't be 100% sure that the enterprise is going to fly. And – sorry to take a pessimistic look at things – if you realize that it's not going to fly after three months, you've still go to pay the lease. I could go on, but you get the point.

What about reversing the process and making the premises idea the second stage of development after the website has proved its worth? Use all that money you're saving for PR, advertising and promotion. Make it possible to buy products off the page of a newspaper or specialist magazine advertisement. Gear up the website so that you can advertise to make people go to the site and buy online. Then when you're sure you've got a goer, move to the next stage and lease or buy premises.

The other delightful thing about selling products without a shop is that you may not need to buy in stock until you've made a sale – another great saving of cash. Keep sight of the objective: you're aiming to make a million pounds and you want the most cost-effective and least risky route to achieving that aim.

There are lots of Internet millionaires – people who have made a lot of money from selling through the Internet or developing a site that people will pay to visit. The 'dot-com revolution' may be best remembered for its spectacular crash, but don't forget that there are now many more ways of reaching your market than opening a shop.

Let's take a moment to think about some of the issues involved in running your business, maybe an online business, from home. For many people working from home is a lifestyle thing. Gone are the rush-hour traffic jams and missed buses and trains. Instead you only have to wander through to the spare room, sorry office, and you can always answer the office phone in your jim-jams if you decide to read the papers in bed or just have a long lie-in that morning. But experienced home workers have found a few items of best practice and they follow them every day.

Here's the experience of a couple who first set up business in a small flat with no spare room. Within six months not only could they hardly get into the sitting room for papers and files, but also the boots of both their cars were full of office stuff. It is extraordinary how much space you use up to run a business, so allocate yourself the maximum space you can, consistent with the family still having a life, rather than the minimum you could manage with.

It is highly desirable to have a whole room for the business. This is for two main reasons: you are bound to expand; and you need to be able to shut the door on your office at the end of the day. Try not to let things spill over into the living area of the house. I know another couple who work from home in two separate offices. They make their working areas strictly out of bounds for their young children. When the baby-minder is there during the day, they actually communicate with each other by e-mail to avoid going through the living area and being distracted by the children. They advocate that home workers need to be even more expert at time management than office workers, and suggest going on a course about time management if that's a weakness of yours.

They have strict rules about starting and finishing times. They ban weekend work and generally simulate a situation where their office could be in a different town, let alone building. When the kids are grown up you can be more selfish – one of the great advantages of working from home is you can do your work whenever you want. One of my colleagues, for example, works every Saturday morning and goes fishing during the week when the river banks are quieter.

FINDING THE RIGHT PREMISES

If you've thought everything out and you're still convinced that the right way to go is to get your own place, here's how you go about it. In order to work out the detailed costs for the first year of your business, the first step is to find premises. From there you can plan what has to be spent to prepare it for business and how much you will have to pay in rent, rates, insurance and so on as part of the expenses of the business.

The estate agents' mantra is 'location, location, location', and there's a great deal of truth in that when you're looking for your first outlet. It's amazing what you can do with any building – you can expand it, change the layout, completely alter its appearance and so on – but you can't change its location.

So how do you set about finding the right location? Obviously you start at the estate agents or on the Internet searching for premises that might be suitable and are for lease or sale. (Later on in the chapter I'll talk about leasing or purchasing and the implications of the two methods.)

SUGGESTION BOX

As you know by now, I am a great believer in picking the brains of any expert who has knowledge that might be useful and that I can process, file and possibly act on. Good estate agents, used to dealing with commercial properties, have experience that you don't have at the moment. Talk to them about your requirement and your idea. During a recession you will have their undivided attention, remember. If it's a national chain of agents, they may be able to put you in touch with the owners of similar businesses who are far enough away not to feel threatened by what you're intending to do. Ask the agent for names and contact details of people they've sold leases to in the local area and what their experience has been in terms of getting a business going. You're particularly looking for businesses in the general area that you have in mind. So when you're looking for information about an area estate agents can be very helpful and – guess what – the advice is free unless you do business through them! Always go to more than one, of course; and as with all potential suppliers, make sure that they know you're talking to one or two of their competitors as well as them.

It's really vital at this point to keep in the front of your mind what the property is for. Properties and locations can have very emotional overtones. If you love a property and can envision the business of your dreams inside it, watch out that you don't lose your objectivity. In the end, the premises are only there to support your business and allow you to make a million pounds; they're not there for you to enjoy and admire. There's a lot more justification for falling in love with a building when you're buying a house. You go overboard for the place, really want to live there and your negotiating skills go out of the window. You believe any old stuff the estate agent comes up with about other offers that have been made and you probably over-stretch yourself. We've all done it with our dream home; but you mustn't do it in business. After all, if all goes well, you'll be relying on managers all over the place to suggest appropriate premises; you don't have to love each and every one of them. The decision on premises is very, very important. That's why I always kept the actual decision to myself, although I was not averse to good ideas on the topic.

Anyway, what business are you in? If you're in the property business, buy properties, remembering that recent times have proved that property prices are not a one-way street – they go down as well as up. If you're trying to build a business that passes on your passion for its products, services and experience to paying customers, keep that firmly in mind as you tramp the streets.

To begin with, of course, your outlet will be pretty dependent on the people who are passing by the premises – the footfall. You may be hoping that word of mouth and advertising will quickly make people want to travel miles to become your customers, but that's for later. To begin with you need the people passing by and those who work in the area at least to come into the premises to try them out, and then to become regular customers. This differs by type of outlet, of course. If yours is a very specialist outfit, maybe people will travel miles to find you, but a restaurant or a bar needs footfall.

You can do this research academically by studying the demographics of the area. This can be a very useful exercise. You can find out the age of the people walking by, what their average income is, where they tend to live and so on. All of this is available from various companies who specialize in providing such information to companies big and small. But it's expensive and it doesn't remove the absolute necessity for you to do a lot of footwork yourself. I think you can get a much better feel for the footfall of a location by your own observation and by talking to people. In fact, you mustn't let the computerized information of the kind agencies will give you interfere with your gut feel.

Walk down the street at different times of the day and take notes of the sorts of people you're meeting. Speak to them about what they like and dislike about the place, and ask them if they think there's anything missing that they would like to be available to them. Then introduce your idea and see if they agree that there's at least a reasonable chance that they would become a customer. Ask them about lunchtimes: when they take them, what they do and so forth. Many people find this a challenging thing to do, but it's essential. It's part, if you like, of the salesperson/hunter part of the entrepreneur's job. And it's not as difficult as you may think. As long as you smile and give a sensible reason for stopping for a moment, generally people like to talk, particularly about themselves, what they like and what they don't like. (Try not to look like a charity seller or chugger – charity mugger – as I've heard them called.) Dress in the way you would expect your customers to dress and then relax: no one wants to talk to someone who looks as though they're rattling their worry beads.

I found that it helped to carry a clipboard so that it made you look more professional and engaged in real market research. When I did that, I found that people were more likely to chat.

You can make up a generalized flyer announcing that you are going to open such-and-such sort of premises in this area. You can even put a date to it if you like: you're not actually entering into a contract with people, you're just doing your market research. Use sex if you can. Cajole or bribe your friends, particularly pretty young women, to ask the questions and give out the flyers for you. OK, I know that may sound slightly sexist, but it's not just my opinion, it's a recognition of the fact that people are more likely to stop to talk to pretty women than to the local winos you could get to do it for two cans of Special Brew. Besides which, you're trying to make a million, for goodness' sake, not to advance any political cause.

I've sat in my car for hours just studying who goes by. Count the footfall passing the possible premises for two minutes in every twenty and you'll get a reasonable idea of the number of people going by. Use more than one people-counter for this and you can get an idea of the different market types that are involved. Click one counter for a person over 40, another for someone in a suit, and so on. Think it through and make a plan that's suitable for the business you're thinking of putting down there.

Don't forget about car parking. For some businesses it's crucial and can actually be a deal-breaker for some premises if they are to be used by people who need to park to come in. It may sound silly, but owners do it – they put reserved parking signs up in their small car park for the owners and staff. That isn't a good idea – reserve them for your customers.

When you're searching for your second outlet, you're in a much stronger position. You have the success of the first business to guide you to the sort of customers you're chasing. You're also aware of what other services your customers use in the vicinity. I know a very successful chain that has discovered that its best locations occur when there are local cash machines and a branch of Boots nearby.

Now study the other businesses in the area. Which of them are busy and which of them are not? What type of customer goes into them? Again, talk to the owners of the businesses. They're not going to tell you that they're doing very badly, but they will probably say something that goes into the melting pot of information you're trying to gather. As you will certainly do, business owners tend to talk up their businesses and take a very optimistic view, so balance talking to them with talking to their staff – they can reveal a lot in terms of how busy or bored they are.

Then look at the competition: both direct, that is selling the same products to the same markets, and indirect, an alternative way of satisfying the need – people getting breakfast, for example, can eat inside the outlet or take it away. Do they sell their products on a telephone order and delivery basis as well as through the shop, and so on? You've got to be better than these people so you need to know as much detail as possible about how they operate to be able to plan your unique selling proposition.

It is terribly tempting to make a decision too fast on the very important issue of where to site your business. Maybe because you don't do your research well enough, you go for the first place you like, or maybe because the estate agent gives you the 'you've got two competitors for this property' speech, or maybe because you're just aching to get on with it and can't wait. The 'you've got two competitors for this property' speech is always a lie in good times or bad. Don't succumb to any of these drivers – you don't just want a suitable place, you want the best one possible.

A mathematician friend of mine gave me a very interesting trick. If you operate on the basis she recommends, you give yourself the best possible statistical chance of choosing the most appropriate location. Here's how it goes. When you have found a location that would do because it fits the bill reasonably well, in all probability with a few flaws, use it as a benchmark. Then keep looking until you find one that's better and go for that one. If the worst comes to the worst you can always go back to the benchmark property, but at least you've had a really good look. I understood the maths of it when she explained it to me but I can't remember it, and in any case it doesn't much matter – it works. I quite like it since it has a double benefit: it improves the statistical chance of finding the best property available and has the benefit of making you keep looking even when you've found a property that would just about do. Having said that, I probably got to the same conclusion with my common sense rather than maths.

KNOWING YOUR COSTS AND YOUR BREAK-EVEN POINT

You've got to keep your eye on the financial side of your business or, unless you're terribly lucky, you're going to come a cropper. One of the businesses I worked with went for almost eight months without understanding what its financial position was. I persevered and eventually got hold of the figures. I then showed them on a spreadsheet that they were losing about £500 a week and that, if they went on like that, they would have lost well over £20,000 during the first year. I explained how I had come to this conclusion, simply comparing turnover with the operating costs during the period, and one of the partners asked if my figures included the set-up costs. This is a silly question, revealing that she didn't know anything about the financial side of a business.

Sorry folks, you don't have to become an accountant to run your own business, like you don't have to be an electronics engineer to work on a computer spreadsheet, but you can't take the risk of being financially innumerate. Not only will you not be able to monitor your performance, but you'll get stuffed by the folk out there you're dealing with. If your supplier knows more about your profit margins than you do, you're not going to get the best deal. Good salespeople can calculate gross margin in their heads without looking as though they're doing it or missing a beat in their pitch.

A lot of companies shield their employees from real-world finance by only giving them access to management accounting systems. These serve the purpose of giving the board financial control and setting targets for each department. If you only have experience of this kind of system, you may have to bone up on things like break-even analysis and cash flow before you go out on your own. In a big company there's a treasury department looking after the cash flow. That department may require managers to change their objectives from time to time. It may, for example, instigate a big push on getting customer invoices paid more quickly. Managers are therefore involved in keeping the cash flow satisfactory, but this is a lot different from looking after the cash yourself. I've known business entrepreneurs who couldn't work out how to add VAT to an invoice or calculate the tax on a price that includes VAT. That won't do, I'm afraid. Try to get the hang of the basics as you do your planning or you'll learn them the hard way when you suddenly realize, for example, that you're not going to have enough cash to pay the wages.

So what do you need?

You need a budget for fitting out the premises. And you've got to stick to it. If you've allowed 10% for contingencies – costs that you weren't expecting – that is sensible, but after that keep within the budget. Here's another thing that sounds silly but lots of people forget: just because there's money allocated in the budget for something, you don't have to spend it. Perhaps this is another big-company thing, with middle managers feeling compelled to spend their whole budget whatever happens; but if you find a cheaper way of doing something after you've drawn up the budget, take that route. Don't let the money burn a hole in your pocket. It's amazing how quickly even a major input of investment or loan capital can disappear. I know a big company that put in place a training course with the aim of urging managers to spend the company's money as though it were their own. It's easier for you – spend as little as you can because you're not pretending, it is your own money. And yet, I promise I've worked with owners who ignored lower-cost opportunities and went on to spend the money in the budget.

You need accurate knowledge of your overheads: the fixed costs that will occur whether you sell anything or not. Keep that number in your head and when it goes up – for example, when you take on another member of staff – add those costs to the monthly total.

Remember that you have to cover the overheads with the profits you're making from the products you're selling. You don't cover the overheads with the turnover, the money that customers pay; remember the Helsinki. This means that you've got to know the profit you make from the products you sell – the profit margin.

Right, if you know your overheads, and you know the profit margins that your products make, you can work out your break-even point – the point at which the profits you've made on the products you've sold equals the overheads. After that you're making money that belongs to you and you can pay your salary.

If you know the break-even point, you can work out how much the takings, or turnover, have to be for any period of time. Certainly on a monthly basis, possibly on a weekly basis and even on a daily basis, you need to know if you're breaking even. If you're just starting it may be difficult to succeed in that immediately, but keeping tabs on these four things – break-even point, overheads, profit margins on products and daily turnover – gives you a good control of the business. If the turnover drops below break-even you need to know instantly so that you can take action to put it right. We'll talk about controlling cash flow later on.

There's more detail on this in Item 4 in the Entrepreneur's Toolkit, Drawing up the first rough financial plan.

In the early stages we tended to go for the lease of buildings rather than getting a mortgage and buying them. My main argument for doing so was that we were trying to build the business up as fast as we could, and no matter how much money you raise in debt, you've also got to put some deposit money down if you're intent on buying. It's frequently the case that the deposit money could be working for you better elsewhere, either in working capital or as the refurbishment money for the new premises.

As Simon says, 'I always signed every cheque to make sure that we had a complete insight into what was going on.'

DECIDING WHETHER OR NOT YOUR IDEA HAS LEGS

It was very interesting to work with one business where the owners had bought their first premises. They did the refurbishment and opened up their bar/café. After about six months, they were doing OK but not really taking off – and certainly not producing profits that would make either of them a millionaire. They were also working incredibly hard, with at least one of them on the premises all the time; and the business was open long hours, seven days a week. They couldn't go on like they were for ever; they'd either go bust or go mad. But they couldn't expand either by taking on another outlet because they didn't have any money. The deposit and the expenses they had incurred in buying the property had left them borrowed pretty much to the hilt. What was the way ahead? Financially and physically, there's a limit to how long you can run a business at break-even or just above: it's exhausting and there's no light at the end of the tunnel.

This is a situation that a lot of start-ups get into. They're not really making money, and they're certainly not making real money. The owners are probably living on a very small salary, or none at all. And, of course, your lives are not your own: they now belong to the business. If you take your eye off the ball by, for example, having a day off to watch the school concert around Christmas, the till will take less on a crucial day in the retailing year.

So what do you do? First, you work hard on improving things. You look at the competition to see what they're doing differently from you. You try to work out why their premises are busy all day long while you have lulls at different parts of the day. You get feedback from your customers by asking them what they like and dislike about the experience they've just had. Learning from all of this, you tune the look and feel of the premises and perhaps the products on offer. Trade goes up a bit, but you're still hovering round that break-even mark.

You look for cost savings too, but you're probably down to the bone by this stage anyway. You can use the situation to try to get a bit more off your suppliers' prices, but after six months or more in business you've probably got the costs down as far as you can.

At what point will you decide that the concept has a fundamental flaw, take a step back and replan your strategy?

My view is that you must replan when you're still in control of your business. I think there's a pivotal point in most small businesses at about half a year. You haven't run out of money yet, but the accountant has drawn a graph showing that you are within months of that happening. So you're still in control. You could just wait the extra 12 months, watch the constant drip, drip, drip of cash going out and than have the bank step in and tell you what to do. When it does that, it almost certainly means you've risked it all and lost it all.

There is a general view out there that you haven't given a concept enough time until you've tried it for 12 to 18 months, but I like to look at things more practically. Much earlier than that you've had warning signs. Suppose you realize after six months that break-even is still the best month that you ever have. Why wait another year? You're going to have lost even more money; and that's assuming you haven't had a heart attack or a nervous breakdown. You're taking risks with your health and your family life, for goodness' sake – and you haven't even got the compensation of pots of dough.

Look, you're a businessperson. In your heart of hearts you'll know when you've tried everything and still not reached profitability, so don't hang about. Have a radical rethink. Take a step back and have a hard, honest look at things.

Get off the premises for a sensible amount of time to weigh up your position. List your strengths and weaknesses. The strengths will include that you've learnt a lot in several months' experience. You know how to organize builders, buy fixtures and fittings, and design a retail concept. You've learnt how to hire, manage and fire staff and you've grasped the technical part of your particular trade. You own or have a lease on the premises and you've improved them since you took over. You've still got a bit of cash in the bank.

Now look at the next crucial part of the planning process – your weaknesses. Look for a fundamental flaw. If it's the location, stop kidding yourself that somehow, as if by magic, that's going to improve. If it's the concept, admit it – to yourself first of all, then to your friends and advisers. Don't fool yourself into thinking that all will be well when a recession is over. Your business has to make money now. A recession can last for two years or even more.

Now look at your options. What could you do to overcome the weaknesses? Is there a skill you lack that you would learn if you worked for someone else? Think radically and then write down the options you've got. Talk to anyone who can help you to get away from your fixed idea of what you've being trying to do.

The first option is obviously to continue as you are, keep fine-tuning and hope that things pick up. The other options are more radical and probably involve a major change of direction.

It's decision-making time. Which of these options are you going to go with? Remember, a major change of direction is not an admission of failure – it's a decision to stop banging your head against a brick wall.

Back to the bar/café owners. I got them to review their strategy by first looking at their strengths and weaknesses. In the months they had been in business, they had learnt an enormous amount. They knew how to recruit and handle staff; they knew how to organize a kitchen and make sure that the logistics of serving customers were appropriate in terms of portion, price and speed of service. These are all very valuable lessons and an important 'soft' asset for any business. The owners could transfer those skills anywhere if they had the money to start an expansion programme.

Now, if they could sell the premises they'd bought as a going concern, they'd probably get at least as much as they'd paid and spent on it, and perhaps a bit more. With that release of capital they could lease at least two new outlets, repeat the refurbishment process (probably much more efficiently the second time round) and expand their business. That would also mean that they could bring in a manager for each bar/café and release themselves from the drudgery of a life of serving, sleeping and not a lot else. We were talking in the days when property was relatively easy to sell. When it isn't, the argument for not buying in the first place becomes even stronger. I'm definitely not saying that a buy decision is always wrong; on the contrary, we made a lot of money by buying freeholds. But think hard about the implications, particularly to your expansion plans, and particularly in the early stages.

The topic of 'buy or lease' brings up lots of interesting business practices, such as measuring return on assets, discounting cash flows and so on. You might like to have a look at these in Item 5 in the Entrepreneur's Toolkit, The decision to lease premises or buy them.

PAPER TALK

During the shooting of *Risking It All*, I'd advised a family who'd bought a run-down hotel in Dorset to invest their way out of trouble. They were perilously in debt, but I urged them to borrow another £150,000 to get their place into shape. My bullish advice was lapped up and they hurled themselves further into debt. It made great TV.

The problem is that we filmed that sequence when interest rates were low. After that interest rates moved up and the housing market stalled. Frustratingly, interest rates then plummeted, but it's now hard to get a loan at a low rate. I'm not a pessimist, but one of the advantages of being over 40 is that I've seen the signs before and know what they presage, so I can take action perhaps a little bit before less experienced people would.

We've had a long period of relatively low interest rates and they have now gone down even further, but it still pays to check your plan against the possibility that they might go up, a little in the short term and significantly in the long run. There is a view that the governments of the world spending their way out of recession will cause big inflation problems when the upturn does take place.

4

THE OPENING DAYS

The opening of your premises is a very important time. It's your opportunity to induce people to try out something new. In this chapter we'll cover:

- Thinking about the marketing and networking side of the enterprise
- Getting it busy quickly at start-up time
- Making sure that the first impression your premises give your customers and potential customers is exactly the one you want
- Writing a detailed business plan

PLANNING THE MARKETING PROCESS

The main reason new small businesses don't succeed is because they don't get enough customers – it's as simple as that. It's said that if you invent a better product, no matter how simple it is, people will beat a path to your door to buy it; but that's not my experience. It's hard graft that fills retail outlets and brings customers to service business and websites. You've got to put aside a certain amount of time on a regular basis to tell people about your business and entice them in.

We carried out our own marketing campaign to launch the new business. This was mainly by word of mouth, although we did give out thousands of fliers in university areas. We talked to hundreds of people about what we were going to do. In the end, word of mouth was a massive help because it works like a pyramid, but it doesn't happen by itself; you've got to work hard to get the snowball rolling. Opening day was packed, partly because the bar was fashion-led – the music, the ambience and the look and feel hit the current hot buttons, so the venue was right. It was also packed because we had worked hard at telling people all about it. We learnt later that this is called networking and it's a very useful and simple technique; its only requirement is energy and discipline. There were our friends, friends of our friends, and friends of our friends' friends – you get the picture. We gave away a lot of drinks that day and got the bar busy and, to our great relief, it stayed busy. We called this technique 'rent a crowd'. You bribe a load of people to come in by offering bargains, in our case cheap drinks. Once you've got a crowd in, it's easy to get the others to follow.

We tried to be adventurous and innovative on the product and customer-experience side as well, concentrating on distinguishing our venue from all the others in Brighton. For example, on the product side we offered flavoured vodka shots. We put sweets into the dishwasher to turn them into a liquid, added them to vodka and froze them to make a new type of drink that people told their friends about. It was something new and you could only buy them in our bar. This was marvellous, because it meant that we could charge a premium for a product that didn't cost us much to make. We offered two-for-one deals at appropriate times; this suited the customers because it was great value, and it suited us because it filled the venue at times of the day that were normally slow.

We did, as I look back on it now, take some quite big risks, ones that I'm not sure I would take now. For example, we launched a promotion called 'Pop your Pils' aimed at selling more Pilsner lager.

The joke was a play on the vogue at that time of taking ecstasy in clubs and was an in-joke for the demographic we were trying to attract. It was pretty risky, as it could be seen as showing an irreverent attitude to what many people saw as a major problem. It was a risk, too, from the point of view of our relations with the police, as it could have been seen as advertising the fact that E was available, or at least that we were not taking the issue as seriously as we might. But guess what? It worked, and our sales of Pilsner and other products went through the roof. It's amazing what you can get away with if you think innovatively and take a few risks.

Perhaps most importantly, we kept up the marketing side too, publicising our venture incessantly with fly-posting and letterbox drops. Fly-posting is illegal and, on one occasion, Simon realized he was going to be caught in the act and jumped into a skip. Unfortunately, he was spotted and arrested. Although he was eventually let off, it just goes to show that if you are serious about doing your own publicity – as we were – it can involve certain dangers.

We networked with student unions and university clubs and societies offering sponsorship of football teams at both universities.

We got the place looking just as our customers wanted it – with an emphasis on making a knockout first impression. Think about the first impression people will get of your new premises; it's desperately important.

Simon was big on talking up the company. Whatever turmoil we were going through, we always kept an air of coolness. We talked about the company as though it were a major concern years before it did in fact become a major concern. As I have said, 'We're doing pretty well in difficult circumstances' is a better message to give out than 'Like all businesses we are close to being in trouble', no matter what the recession has made of the true situation.

THEY ONLY DO IT ONCE – GET A FIRST IMPRESSION, THAT IS

The presentation of your outlet or website can be compared to speed dating. Potential customers eye you up and, almost instantly, decide whether or not they're interested in taking things further. So, you need to be able to build rapport with your customers as quickly and effectively as possible. Cliché it may be, but you never have a second chance to make a first impression.

Start with the look of your place. What does it communicate to a person seeing it for the first time? Try to put yourself in the shoes of a typical customer and look at the place from every angle, at different times of the day. Look at it from across the street, approaching from the left, approaching from the right and crossing the street to come at it full on. Listen to what it's saying to you.

First of all there are some rules for all premises, no matter what product or service they supply:

- Is it welcoming? Does it look comfortable and non-threatening? Does it look as though I'll have a relaxed and pleasant experience if I go in? In some premises there are particular obstacles to making a positive first impression. For example, if your stock is fragile, you have to deal with the risk of breakages – people touching or picking up glass and porcelain objects in a shop may be a real cause for concern. In such situations you'll have to contend with the possibility of people damaging the goods. But then you'll have to weigh this up against putting people off from entering your shop altogether. I once went into an upmarket gift shop where the owners had put up a great number of signs saying 'Do not touch', 'All breakages must be paid for' and so on. The overwhelming impression was that I was not welcome – that my presence was a threat to their business, not to mention my own wallet. I was almost too scared to breathe!

- Is the first thing a customer sees on entering the premises what you want them to base their first impression on? Entrance halls – even very small areas around the doorway – are the first signal of what your customers can expect. I've seen such areas used for storage or taken up by a huge untidy pile of outdoor clothes; not what you want.

- Is it spotlessly clean? There is absolutely no excuse for any dust or dirt. Don't stint on cleaning; mess and dirt are probably the biggest turn-offs of the lot. Make sure everyone who works with you knows that clearing up the remains of the last customer is part of their job description. It's not just the waiters who pick up the dirty crockery, it's everyone: chef, manager or owner. A table that hasn't been cleaned is a grave danger to first impressions, so make the time that it's in that state as short as possible. Hair on the floor in the hairdressers, clothes still off the hangers in the clothes shop and bottles out of order in the display of grooming products – all are very bad news.

- Does the customer quickly understand the range of goods and services on offer? By all means have some eye-catching pictures, some beautiful but unrelated sculptures or whatever; but don't hide the fact of what you are. It can be very confusing if the décor suggests that the outlet offers something it doesn't.

- A-boards are very useful and, if well-designed, can give a great first impression and entice passers-by to your door. You can be innovative here as well. I know of a bar/bed-and-breakfast place that stands close to the boundary of two counties. The owner put up an A-board on the main road and found that it attracted quite a lot of passing traffic (literally, you might say). Unfortunately, the bar was close to the county town of the county in which it lay and a planning officer spotted the sign and told him to remove it. He didn't remove it but he did move it – to the other side of the county line. This was a long way from the planning officers of the second county, and the board is still there.

- Do the colours you use attract the sort of customers you want? There are masculine colours and feminine colours; there are adult colours and children's colours. If you don't know much about what colours say, ask someone who does or consult a book or a website. For example, www.colour-affects.co.uk is a very useful site, offering advice such as: 'if you are selling baby clothes, or toys, everyone entering the shop is thinking in terms of infancy, parenthood and childhood – even if they themselves are grandparents. We would not suggest crude primaries, but a colour scheme that subtly reminds people of these concepts. If, on the other hand, your retail outlets are bank branches, betting shops, high-fashion stores or anything else, the colours must appeal to different parts of the customers' psyche.' However, don't go mad or take risks. While there is certainly truth in this paragraph, if you go into too much depth you could end up aiming at too small a group of people. The colours have to work for the whole range of your customers. I would advocate adopting a middle-of-the-road course: not too fashionable, trendy or risky. There's always a palette of colours that is fashionable. Make sure you know what these colours are at any one time by looking at the appropriate magazines: *Elle Decoration* and suchlike.

- One quick point about product layout: generally speaking, women are happy to forage in shop displays to find what they want. They're happy to browse through a full rack of dresses to find one they like, and they're quite happy to leave behind a trail of disturbed displays for other people to put right. Men want everything laid out in front of them. If they have to move something to see something else, they probably won't, and they hate disturbing displays. This means that you have to find cleverer ways of presenting products to men, making really good use of the space you've got to display everything they can buy. I find that people are generally pretty unobservant. Make things as obvious as you can – you can't make them stick out too much.

My first meeting with two people thinking of setting up a shop for men's grooming and treatment was an eye-opener in this respect. They chose the shop because so many outlets in the vicinity were 'destination shops'. A destination shop is one that people seek out and travel to, rather than drop in to casually because they are passing by or it's close to home or work. And many of these neighbours were male-oriented outlets too.

They had a piece of luck with the next-door shop. It was a men's clothes store aimed pretty much at the same market as theirs. Its outside colours were quite neutral, which suited them, and they obviously took that into account when planning their own scheme.

The premises for their shop were in a fairly narrow London street with high buildings on either side. One important consideration was that the shop front was on the shady side of the street – and people have a tendency to walk on the sunny side. This meant that most people would form their first impression, and decide whether to stop and look or go in, from the opposite side of the street. One argument goes, 'That means that they take in the whole premises in their first impression, rather than being close up to it, which is a good thing.' The counter to that is, 'Yes, but the look of your shop has to persuade them to cross the street.' It's a fair debate, but given the choice I'd always go for the sunny side of the street.

One of the best examples of giving exactly the first impression they wanted was a male grooming shop in Carnaby Street, London, a fabulous venue for such a venture. The shop just said 'blokes' from the moment you saw the window, which included a display centred around a heavy, metal trunk of the sort you see in Formula One racing pits. It continued saying 'blokes' with the first counter you met, which had on it a *Playboy*-style book with Marilyn Monroe on the cover. This first counter also displayed a pair of designer moccasins.

Grooming products were displayed at head height round the shelves on all three walls of the shop. There was also an Aladdin's cave of desirable and funky objects – from expensive chunky watches to false moustaches. The owners had really thought about their customers and produced a masculine atmosphere that wasn't in the least intimidating or off-putting, given that male grooming products are still a bit iffy for a lot of men, who don't like asking for them or talking about them.

Add to this the well-trained staff, who knew the grooming products inside out, and you have a recipe for success. I would challenge most men to go in there and not buy something, and it didn't surprise me to learn that the average customer spend in that shop was about £70. I learnt a lot from visiting this shop – a lot about getting inside customers' heads and offering something that will attract them in and make them buy.

FIRST IMPRESSIONS OF A WEBSITE

If the key to finding premises is location, location, location, the key to a website in my view is navigation, navigation navigation. You cannot work this out for yourself. You may find the way you have set your site up to be entirely logical and easy to use, but until you have tested it with a lot of people you will never know what an outside person's reaction will be. Again, listen to everything the testers say. They may be wrong and you do not have to change the website to make it exactly how they want it, but their view is terribly important, so listen up.

Get one or both of your parents to try the site out. That's the great thing about selling from a website: people can visit it when you are in the UK and they're in New Zealand. Test it to destruction. Remember the first impression rule: if customers don't get on with your site in about two minutes they will abandon the attempt and buy somewhere else.

The good news is that an awful lot of websites, particularly those of small businesses, are absolutely terrible and cause frustration at the exact point they should be causing buying feelings. Once again, there is no substitute for research. Try out a whole load of websites yourself, work out the ones you can get on with and 'borrow' their techniques. Learn and copy.

AND SO TO THE PEOPLE

How often have you got your first impression of a company or a retail outlet from what people tell you about it? The answer is probably many times. Indeed, word of mouth is the cheapest and most effective kind of advertising and promotion you can get. But how often have you heard someone say, 'Oh, the people are really friendly and helpful.' Probably not as often, and certainly not as often as you've heard something like, 'I couldn't believe how they treated us. They made us feel really awkward because we were only having a drink.' This is not because most outlets have rude or unfriendly people. It's because nowadays you're only playing for a draw with your competitors if properly

SUGGESTION BOX

Plan for how your staff will appear in terms of what they're wearing as well as how they behave towards your customers. It has to be consistent with the brand and first impression you're trying to create. The owners of one café/bar I worked with originally dressed their staff in quite smart uniforms, but in first impression terms they stuck out like sore thumbs. The ambience they were trying to create was one of informality and easy relaxation. In this almost continental appearance, which is what they were aiming at, the staff looked more at home in a station or on a train. The uniforms were inconsistent with the experience they wanted their customers to have. They soon abandoned them and moved to a very casual form of dress that suited their brand and environment much better.

Remember, if you don't provide the clothes your staff will wear, they are more or less on a daily basis making a decision about your brand. Either talk long and hard to them about how you want them to look or bite the bullet and invest in the clothes you want them to wear.

trained and attentive staff are delivering a high standard of customer service.

OK, back to our first successful pub. Turnover and profit allowed us to recover the cost of the refurbishment in three months. We didn't pay back the loan, of course, because it wasn't due; but crucially, neither did we spend the money as we had with the Helsinki – we left it in the business.

The only downside to this, and it was easy to fix, was the discovery that running a business with four equal partners doesn't make sense; so Simon and I bought out the other two. They were happy because they made a good profit on their original investment. We set up the new business with the rather sonorous title Webb Kirby Ltd. This was the first time we used purchasing equity to solve a problem – but it certainly wasn't the last.

WARNING: THINGS TO WATCH OUT FOR

Don't have too many partners – four is too many, two is better. It's simply too difficult to get agreement if there are four people with equal shares, not only because people have different views and can argue them cogently, but also because of the logistics – you need to make a quick decision on a supplier and, guess what, one of the partners is on holiday and the other's at a funeral in Scotland. And then, because you can't agree on a particular course of action, there have to be compromises, and before you know it you've got a committee running your business. (Committees are the ones that breed sub-committees like rabbits and eventually design the camel, and a watch that looks and feels great but doesn't actually make it easy to tell the time.)

THE NEXT OUTLET

Right, you're doing well. You've proved that your original idea, probably with a bit of tuning, does work. You've made your place busy and you have a plan for how to keep it busy by advertising, promotions and other marketing activities. You've set time aside every day to think about and get involved in marketing the product to a wider and wider audience. (And I mean every day. Make a point of asking yourself at the beginning of each day, 'What am I going to do today that will increase the number of customers coming into my premises or increase the profit that I make from each one that does come in?') You've also got a lot of very valuable experience that you can use as you expand the business.

You know enough about your profit margins to be able to plan your pricing and the costs of your products. You're making money. You're working very hard, because there's always something to be done and you've got to keep up the amount of time you spend on site, but then hard work comes with the territory.

You should now be confident that you can become a millionaire; because it's true, you can. But as I've said, you've got to expand the business and the idea. So you're looking for new premises and starting the process again.

You know the one about the famous old golfer Arnold Palmer who spoke to a spectator after he'd just pulled off an incredible bunker shot from a badly plugged lie? The spectator said, 'You were lucky there, Arnie,' and Arnie replied, 'Yes, and the harder I practice, the luckier I get.' I have found this to be true in my entrepreneurial life. As I've got more and more experienced, bits of luck do come my way.

And we had a bit of luck with our second outlet. We had got the first place really buzzing, we were making money, we were leaving it in the business – and at this point, a brewery approached us with an offer to take over one of their bars. Why did we get this unexpected opportunity? What made us attractive to the brewer? First and foremost, they liked our energy and our innovation. And, would you believe, we had what all start-up entrepreneurs yearn for – a track record. We also had enough experience to be able to put a pretty respectable and realistic plan in place. The proposition was attractive to us because we'd noticed something unique about the location. The pub was situated at a point at which students walking into Brighton from the two main universities converged. It was potentially an ideal meeting point for young people walking into town. We used the geographic benefit to great effect and the pub became a frequently used first stopping place on a night out.

ARGH! NOT THE BUSINESS PLAN

At some point we've got to address the dreaded business plan. I call it the dreaded business plan because in my mind a lot of business plans can easily miss the point. Even the forms that banks make you fill in when you want to borrow money can hide the fact that you don't really know what your business vision is. They're strong on detail and have enough spreadsheets to make your nose bleed, but they don't necessarily include the overriding vision and strategy for the business. So, to make a million, you need a clear vision of the product you are taking to market, now and into the future. You also need a strategy for what needs to be done to work as fast as possible on expanding the business.

You can actually keep this information in your head or on the back of a cigarette packet, which is how I do it. But you will probably need a written business plan and lots of people feel more comfortable if they've gone through some form of process to document their plan. Let me say first and foremost that, whatever hoops bankers and other lenders and investors make you jump through in terms of document-ing your plan, you can actually do it very briefly and informally. In fact, the informal plan has the benefit of taking up much less writing-chore time, which means that you have more time for the interesting and important part of the plan – thinking the issues through and taking common-sense decisions. But at this stage in your business life you probably need to borrow money, so I've included an example of the forms that bankers want in Drawing up a detailed business plan – Item 6 in the Entrepreneur's Toolkit.

Bankers will insist that your plan covers three years in detail, and years four and five in outline. I personally find three years not just long, but way too long; however, it may be useful, provided you keep going back to the three-year plan and revising it in the light of actual performance. And I tend not to give much away in my long-term plan, so years four and five look pretty much like a continuation of the previous year with 10% added everywhere. It saves time, and it's probably as accurate as trying to work out what will really happen, particularly if you're always looking for new opportunities – you can't plan for them until they pop up.

I became legendary with the people who worked for us for my catchphrase 'Lights down, music up'. This was a simple formula that could make even the worst pub better very quickly. So there you have it – the key to any business can be summed up in two or three killer points.

SUGGESTION BOX

'Suits' in their 50s like to work with young enthusiasts. Unwieldy businesses can tap into the energy of the young, and effective managers in their 40s and 50s know this. You must really exploit this to get the best deal you can from investors, bankers, suppliers, customers – everyone. Always look enthusiastic, keen and cheerful, even when your back's against a financial wall. People a good bit older than you then start to trust that if you agree to do something, it will actually happen; something that is not necessarily true in their own bureaucratic organizations.

And it works the other way round as well. If you're already an older person when you start, look out for some cool, sharp young people to employ. That's what I do now.

When the brewery offered us the lease, the pub was mainly patronised by elderly men. After all, it was being run by someone of retirement age and customers look for their like when they choose a landlord. Once again we did the refurbishment ourselves, kitted the pub out for a younger clientele and named it the Leek and Winkle. Within three months it became the most profitable student venue in the town.

Then we got a massive break. We bought the lease of the Fortune of War on Brighton seafront. At the time the seafront was quite run-down. It had that 'kiss me quick' feel about it, with tacky souvenir shops and old-fashioned fast-food joints like the worst type of fish-and-chip shop. The landlord of the pub at the time was reaching retirement age and he didn't like his pub to be too busy. This gave us an excellent negotiating position with the brewery, as by this time we had the experience to know that the turnover he was getting was a lot less than the potential of the site. It was indeed a massive break – we bought the lease for £50,000 and during the second week of trading took £50,000. We actually made the front page of the *Sun* newspaper. We called the newsdesk and told them we had sold 20,000 pints in one day when the weather was hot and bingo – with no further checking the good old *Sun* printed it as fact. To be fair, the actual figure – about 5000 – was pretty impressive as well.

This, I would say, put us on the map. Breweries were all interested in what we were doing, and the young population of Brighton had identified what they thought were a few ideal watering holes. Again, we were able to exploit the breweries' interest by playing one off against the other, not only in terms of the price at which they offered us products, but also with mutual offers and promotional campaigns. We were pretty aggressive with the competition. We put 20 attractive young people on the streets to hand flyers to people approaching a competitor's club. No one could actually get into that club without receiving a free drink voucher for our venue. It's very similar to Tesco offering special deals that make life very difficult for the corner shops.

Let's finish this bit off by looking at a cautionary tale of a business that lost touch with its customers. Somehow, whatever key strategic ideas the board formulated, they just didn't work. I wrote about Airfix in a *Daily Telegraph* article and included this extract.

PAPER TALK

There can be few blokes of my generation who haven't derived some childhood pleasure from Airfix kits. They taught us patience, dexterity and a great deal about history. At least that's what the media hype on this sad topic would have you believe. The argument I've read several times is that Airfix is just too boring for today's 'shoot 'em up' generation. They'd rather be lowering their IQs on console games than sticking bits of plastic together to represent ancient bombers.

Someone has missed the point. For me, the fun of Airfix wasn't in making the kits. It was in chucking them out of windows, setting fire to them and shooting them with my air rifle. I even confess to trying to blow up the odd Heinkel or Messerschmitt. The invention of ever more realistic and gruesome crash scenarios for my model aeroplanes warmed the cockles of my boyish heart. Airfix tapped into every lad's innocent obsession with blood, bombs and guns. Boys will be boys, after all.

For my generation, Airfix represented something just as bloody and violent as the modern computer games that we love to criticize today. So why are Airfix doing so badly? After all, I'm pretty sure boys are much the same today as they were 30 years ago.

Shortly after this article, Hornby bought Airfix. Hornby has been clever. It's managed to appeal to a new generation while retaining its existing customers. It refers to its older customers as 'enthusiasts'. With the help of Harry Potter's Hogwarts Express and a commitment to quality, it's become Europe's largest model railway manufacturer. It's continued to understand its market as the environment changes and altered its vision accordingly. I hope it does the same for Airfix.

SUGGESTION BOX

It's easy, if costly, to make a business busy. Pack it out by offering crazy deals, perhaps at certain times of the day. People are interested in busy premises – the 'What's going on there?' syndrome. Nothing attracts people to come in as much as a venue that is buzzing with your type of person. Whether it's a bar or an art gallery, passing trade want to feel that they won't be on their own if they go in. And it's human nature to wonder if you're missing something if you pass a shop with lots of smiling people milling around – nobody wants to miss a bargain or a new fashion.

So here's my suggestion. Look around at the retail businesses near you and divide them into those that are obviously busy practically all the time and those that are not or have bad slack periods at some point during the day or week. Ask yourself why this should be so. Sometimes it's the nature of the business – the idea is simply not good enough – but often it's because the owners haven't got it quite right. Being able to spot something that's not entirely right is key to getting the customers in and creating a busy atmosphere.

And sometimes it's because the owners are too busy tuning the product to get on with the task of marketing. It's interesting to note that after the businesses in *Risking It All* had been on TV their premises were absolutely rammed – reasonable return for the hard work involved in talking for hours and hours to me, the camera crew and director.

BUILDING ON SUCCESS

Right, you've got the business going. You understand your market and how to reach it, but you're still not able to find an exit strategy that will make you your first million. Perhaps the time has come to press down on the accelerator and grow the business. In this chapter we'll look at how our business snowballed, what we learnt during that phase and the following key issues:

- Expanding premises-based businesses
- Hiring the best people to assist with the management of the business
- Motivating the people who deal with your customers
- Mixing and matching appropriate management styles
- Presenting your business as substantial, not an upstart

BUILDING FAST

If you've really got your garage-based business making money and you're using an effective Internet-based shopping system, you may need to expand your advertising and promotion to take the next few steps towards your first million. Then you need to expand your ware-housing and probably spend on software development to mark the route ahead. In a retail business, perhaps you've got your second outlet up and making money. Who knows, you might already be worth over a million pounds; perhaps you've started the first franchise and that's making you money too; but if you're going to find a way of cashing in your chips, you've probably got to do more. This means looking for more premises and putting in management processes that make sure that your managers and staff are equipped to succeed.

During the next two years our business snowballed. We added another site every three months. We had evolved a good process for doing this. We both tended to do the searching for new sites, and when we'd found one and I was happy that it was a real possibility, Simon would run the sliderule over its costs and we would discuss and agree its potential. We got local builders and trades people in and used our, by now, pretty extensive experience to make sure we got a good deal. We actually used the same firm for more than 12 years. By the end of that period they were as knowledgeable about how we wanted the premises to look and feel as we were. There's a huge value in building close relationships with people like this. For a start, it saves so much time – after a pretty cursory look round a new site for about an hour they knew what we were trying to achieve. It also saves money – you don't need expensive makeover experts and interior designers if you've developed a good eye yourself and you've got a builder who can more or less read your mind.

We tried never to give money to middlemen if it was at all possible for us to go direct to the source of the materials and labour we needed. Still bearing in mind the Helsinki fiasco, we financed it ourselves as far as we possibly could. By the end of those two years we had twelve sites all doing pretty well and with nothing that could be described as a failure – that was still to come – and we were continuing to live on subsistence wages. Sorry to go on about it, but every pound you spend on yourself is a pound less to expand the business.

I'm not saying you shouldn't enjoy some of the trappings of a professional and successful entrepreneur, but you still haven't built a business that someone is prepared to value and buy. We maybe took this to an extreme because of the Helsinki, but it's a good lesson nevertheless.

You may also have to wait out the recession before the time comes to make a decent pile out of selling the business. Having said that, all the franchises that deal in food and entertainment are doing well during the recession and will probably be a target for people like the private equity funds who are sniffing around for anything that looks as though it will continue to be successful. Interestingly, they are also looking for much smaller businesses than they were when credit was easy and they could borrow money for a short term, buy a business and then sell it on.

If you have a similar experience to us, there will come a time when your business grows very seriously and you realize that you are now running a substantial business with responsibility for a lot of people. The success of your employees in running sites that you can only get to from time to time is crucial to the success of the whole enterprise. So let's talk about how to get the best out of them.

Start at the top. At this level, always hire the best people you can find and afford. Because you're greedy for good ideas, it's got to be right to get people around you who will contribute useful opinions, not only on the business as it is but also on the business as it may become, and on its competitors. So, hire outstanding people and listen to their views, and if you find they're not so outstanding, don't hesitate to get rid of them. Everyone takes a different angle on a business and how it's serving its customers. If you've got a marketing manager or an accountant who's prepared to really understand the business, you've got a great source of ideas for the future.

And the good news during a recession is that there a lot of very good people looking for a new challenge. While I do not like giving equity in my businesses away, you may want to take the opportunity to take on some very good people at lower than market rate in exchange for a share in the business. Remember that share options do not start from 10% – offer someone 2% to begin with and see how it goes. They need a job.

I got a lot of ideas when doing the shoots for *Risking It All*. It is terribly interesting to go from retail outlet to outlet and talk about the look and feel of the new businesses. I frequently discussed my first impressions of the place with the owners and their staff and compared it to how they thought they were presenting their premises. To be fair, it's always difficult when you've set up the place exactly in accordance with your dream, then someone comes along and says that bits of it don't work. It's human nature to respond by defending the decisions you've made. It may be human nature, but it's not the best reaction. In the end it didn't matter a hoot what I thought of their premises, so trying to persuade me that I was wrong and they were right didn't make much sense. But the lesson is that when your managers, customers and others give you feedback, always welcome it, ask for further information and reflect long and hard on what they've said. You don't have to do what they suggest, but it's always worth giving it some thought; and, if you're open-minded enough, you'll probably improve the next customer's experience by making adjustments based on the feedback you're getting.

There was one classic in the TV series when my easy-on-the-purse-strings approach made me recommend that a couple invest much less money than they were planning to on fitting out their retail outlet. They were going to import very flash Italian counters and fittings and I felt that they could do it much more cheaply using local labour.

They listened and then did exactly what they'd dreamt of doing – they went with the Italian job. And guess what, I had to eat a bit of humble pie because the stuff looked absolutely great. I still think they could have produced the same effect for a lot less money, but the first impression customers got from the shop was exactly what the owners had in mind. Well done them. Nevertheless, the financial facts got them in the end and they had to get out of the business.

GETTING THE RIGHT PEOPLE TO DO A GREAT JOB

At the sharp end of the business, where your people are in direct contact with your customers, you've got to start with the right people. Ideally, you want people who are charismatic, good with customers and dedicated to providing them with a first-class service. You can motivate such people quite easily. Just make sure that they feel loved. OK, I know that's quite a strong word, but it's the one that comes nearest to what I'm trying to say. The people who work for you need to feel important and part of the team. Just as you hired them because they smile a lot, so you must smile at them and hold friendly conversations about their lives outside as well as inside work.

And don't forget to show your appreciation. You can't overestimate its importance – it's a key factor in keeping people working hard and smart. So try to remember that people work for money but do a bit extra for recognition, praise and reward. If you think someone is doing a good job, never forget to tell them. A lot of people leave the big 'thank you' until a task is complete, but it's better to do it all the time when people are working on something and making progress. If for no other reason, you can thank them for doing something that otherwise you would have to do yourself.

People – your staff and your customers – are dominated by emotion. Always reward staff as well as pushing them to do better.

Always think about how your staff are making your customers 'feel' as well as how efficiently they are looking after them.

Don't always visit your premises at the same time every day. That way you make sure everyone knows you and expects you to drop in at any time. I've heard it called 'managing by wandering around'. Whatever you call it, it's very important.

When you're interviewing people, don't just ask about their CV and their experience. Think about asking questions that will help you to discover whether the person is going to fit into the way your business works – the 'culture', if you like. So, if you ask 'What sort of company do you like working for?' and they say 'One that makes me exactly aware of what I've got to do', or if you say 'What sort of thing is important to you in working for a company?' and they answer 'Security', these could be important warning signs if you're looking for people who will take calculated risks and use their initiative. It's worth your while to think about the sort of questions you want to ask, to give you a better understanding of potential employees. Try not to hire someone that you know will have to change their way of working to fit in with the rest of your people; they probably won't. Put a lot of time and thought into finding the right people in the first place. Agencies charge a lot of money if you hire one of the people they present to you; but to get the right person, it's worth spending some cash. Some agencies are great and can save you a lot of time.

I like to ask the question, 'Who do you think are the most important people in a good restaurant/hairdresser/souvenir shop?' If they manage to mention the manager, the chef, the waiters, the stylists and the cleaners without mentioning customers, this will be more revealing than any CV. You might have to give them a bit of help, but they should get what you're aiming at – if they've thought about the business of dealing with customers at all.

In our case we employed graduates who were not quite ready to face the real world. They were, for that reason, happy to work the unsocial hours that running a pub entails, because they knew it wasn't their final job and that eventually they would decide on a real job with a career structure that we simply could not offer them. They didn't want a career with us. By working for us, they were holding on to the lifestyle they had got used to as students. This clinging on to youth is a powerful motivator. We managed to employ a team that lived and breathed our industry, but I have to say the burn-out rate was high.

You shouldn't find this motivating bit of the job too difficult if you're genuinely interested in how people tick and if you can normally work out how to get the best out of them. If you do find it difficult to take an interest in your people, you might be better leaving it to others to manage the motivating of the staff, while you concentrate on the key people at the top. But that's not ideal.

Let's talk about your management team: let's say the manager of your second, third and fourth outlets, and your staff people, the ones working on the finance and marketing side. A good team leader has to change their style of motivating to suit the person they're working with. The main thing I've learnt about influencing and motivating people is that they're all subtly different and that you've got to fit horses to courses.

SUGGESTION BOX – HAVE ONE, FORMAL OR INFORMAL

An area where there's an opportunity for rewarding people is when they come up with a good idea or suggestion. My way of getting to their good ideas was to have a drink with them and ask them questions (*in vino veritas* and all that). It may be better in your business to have a more formal approach and ask people to write down any suggestions they might have for improving the business. If you subsequently implement the suggestion, pay a reward whether in money or goods. Then maybe have an annual prize for the best suggestion of the year. People like to compete and this is an area where you can demonstrate to everyone that someone has made a significant contribution and won.

Think about your natural style of working with people. Mine is a consultative style: influencing people by discussion, asking for their opinion and including them when I'm planning. But it comes out differently for different people. For example, my influence over one key manager in my team consisted almost entirely of listening to her, as she worked out what needed to be done and how to do it. At the end of such a session she had made a good decision, knew she had my support and was well motivated to go back and get on with it.

With another person I found I had to spell things out much more, making suggestions and giving advice. Then there was another person who was very process oriented. I motivated and influenced him by helping him through a simple planning process, for example. He also liked to write everything down, which was good as it saved me doing it. Incidentally, some of the processes he developed for his job were very useful in other parts of the business. I didn't hesitate to introduce them elsewhere and made sure that everyone knew their originator. This is a good illustration of the fact that the best people to suggest better ways of doing things are often the people at the coalface. Get into the habit of listening hard to what they say.

In my experience, people who play hard together work hard together. I've always believed in not stinting on parties and other activities to which you invite the staff as a group. It helps to make your company the focus of people's lives. They talk about it back at the workplace; it takes the stuffiness out of being the boss; and it encourages people to stay loyal to the business. One quick tip if you do this – don't drink too much yourself when you're with the group; that can lead to all sorts of problems.

Make sure that close-knit teams all get on together. In a high-pressure area feuds can break out and are very bad for business. Step in quickly, bang heads together and get the issues resolved. It's much better if you can get them to resolve the issues themselves; but if you have to, make a ruling and then make sure that everyone moves on. Bad feeling causes resentment and people do strange things when they feel wronged.

The other benefit of out-of-hours contact is perhaps surprising, but nevertheless true. The retail business is notorious for people finding ways of pilfering from the stockroom or till. I've found that if people know you as a person from social contacts, they're much less likely to steal from you. I suppose it's the ultimate in demonstrating that you're not a big company with pockets deep enough not to notice or bother about a bit of 'honest shrinkage'. Mind you, some people still steal, whatever you do.

At one point in the building of the C-side company, Simon and I realized that we had built such a party culture within our company that everyone was a heavy drinker. That was scary and we feared building a monster where people working in the bars felt that their work was their hobby. So building a company culture around what you're doing is good, but keep your eye on the bigger picture.

A bit of theory might come in handy here. A lot depends on the circumstances of the business as well. Some people talk about 'push and pull' management styles: push being the 'Do what you are told' or autocratic method; pull the consulting, more democratic way of leading people. I naturally lean towards pull, but when the chips are down I can switch into being more directive if events demand it. Think about what you are naturally, and then work on behaving differently where appropriate.

You need to encourage creativity. Sometimes, for example, it's best to hold back from influencing the team over a decision they're making. If you're too involved in getting them to do what you think is best, you run the risk of stifling their creativity. If you let them get on with it, they can come up with the most amazing insights.

In an ideal world, you should be able to help any person who joins your operation to contribute and become a useful member of the team. If someone is performing unsatisfactorily, give them enough of your time to work out what the problem is and address it through training or, for example, giving them experience in other organizations. In theory, if the poor performance continues, you need to go through the process of warnings, verbal and written, still giving the person the chance to improve for as long as possible. Only when that process is complete should you take the ultimate decision and ask them to leave.

But this is not an ideal world and, if you follow a process like that, you'll probably go bust. It may be fair enough for a big corporation with an HR department, HR processes and so on. But when you have someone who is not pulling their weight in a small but growing enterprise, it can be extremely destructive to the rest of the team and therefore to the business. You've got to act quickly and fire them. It's best to avoid an employment tribunal but, to be honest, tribunals have limited powers and it's not too bad if you have to deal with them. Get poor performers out as quickly as possible.

If you've made a mistake in hiring the wrong person, acting quickly also means that it is less expensive: you can buy yourself out of the problem by offering them an unexpectedly high leaving amount. Getting rid of someone in the first twelve months – more than enough time to see if they fit the bill – costs one month's salary. (Incidentally, if you make a leaving payment a redundancy one, you can pay it gross of tax. This sugars the pill for the person you're firing, but can only be done if you are not going to replace them.) Simon believes that he did most of the firing so that we could keep a 'good cop, nasty cop' routine with staff, and there's an element of truth in that.

If you go into one hairdressing salon that I was involved with, you can feel the friendly and even excited atmosphere that pervades it. The owners lead the way, of course, with a readiness to laugh and joke. There's nothing heavy-handed about their management style and the customers pick up on this joviality and come back for more. It's spot on.

PAPER TALK

I practically burst a blood vessel when I read Antony Worrall Thompson's picky criticism of the influx of Eastern European people currently flooding our hospitality and construction industries. So what if they can't tell the difference between goulash and gratin? Who cares if their English needs a little practice?

As an entrepreneur, these young foreigners are heaven-sent. They want to work. They are polite, keen and respectful. They will work for the minimum wage. There is no type of work at which they will turn up their noses. I cannot express how refreshing this is after years of trying to coax home-grown 'yoofs' into jobs that they obviously feel are beneath them.

The average British teenager is now more likely to approach the workplace with an ambition to appear on *The X Factor* or *Britain's Got Talent* than make a success of life through a commitment to hard work. As we can't all be pop stars or disco divas, there are likely to be some very disappointed boys and girls.

In the past I've employed Aussies, Kiwis and South Africans. They've all been real grafters and helped develop my businesses. But there was always the problem that they were just passing through on a great world tour before heading back to their distant homelands.

Not so the Eastern Europeans. The ones I know are here for good. And for business, that's great news. If we know they're around for more than a few months, we can confidently invest in training; we can bring them on and nurture talent. They're on the bottom rungs at the moment, but watch that space!

I agree that they mangle English pronunciation. It's true that their names could clinch a game of Scrabble. But as a flexible, willing resource for British business, they are invaluable. So celebrity chefs, protectionists and 'little Britain' narrow thinkers, please lay off. We need them just as much as they need our jobs.

IMPROVING THEIR SKILLS

The people you need are bright, smiling, happy people – it's as simple as that. Look for attractive people – not necessarily in looks, but people whom others want to talk to. One more point in this area: you're not looking for brilliant talkers as much as brilliant listeners. Watch out for the very extraverted person who talks a lot without asking questions or listening to the answers – they may not be right for you or your customers. Customers want to talk to the staff, not listen to a monologue. The fact that you've hired the right people is not the end of the story, though. Get them on training courses if that's appropriate and worth the considerable expense; and emphasize at all times the importance of top levels of customer service and staff attitude.

You're probably going to think I bang on about training too much, but the lack of it is such a stopper when it comes to really delighting customers. It only takes one mistake or example of bad service to lose a customer. It's not just the fact that a member of staff lacks the knowledge to assist a customer; it's also that this lack of knowledge of what to do or say can lead to a loss of confidence. And it's a vicious circle. If staff are unsure, they'll excuse themselves to go and ask. If they do this a lot, then customers become impatient, show their impatience and staff confidence continues to fall. If one of your staff has a difficult encounter with an unreasonable customer, who lets rip and has a real go, your staff member may become difficult to train; you may even lose them. You can do a hell of a lot of training in-house. In fact, in most cases you can probably do a much better job than an external training company because you know precisely how you want your people to behave.

Your people can't have too much product knowledge or training in how to deal with the type of customers you're trying to attract. One business I dealt with sold smoothies with a cocktail of different mixes of fruits. They had a problem with the speed with which their staff could serve the customers – it just took too long. The reason was that they had to look at the ingredients of the different products in a very inefficient way. The owners produced a laminated manual and held a training session to get the people up to speed with mixing the products. It encouraged the staff to think about the experience that customers were going through and cut the time from order to service – problem solved.

At one restaurant I worked with, the owners were very knowledge-able about good food. They put an enormous amount of effort into the cuisine and its presentation. In the early days, however, they hired young, relatively inexpensive waiters. They were completely inexperienced and didn't know a crème brûlée from a Cadbury's Creme Egg. And they didn't get the training they needed to change that.

The customers at this exclusive and expensive restaurant were not used to such treatment. They were expecting a level of service consistent with the food and, of course, the price. The owners proved, unintentionally, that even the best restaurant – with wonderful food, beautifully presented – can be let down by untrained staff who are not competent to inform or assist.

So, beware of regarding the job you're asking your people to do as so straightforward that you don't need to sit them down and help them know exactly how you want them to behave. Remember, they don't have the same motivation as you and you need to build on their satisfaction with the job by showing them how to do it well, and congratulating them when they get it right. Once again, that's the whole trick about motivation really – make sure that your people feel loved. Watch out for naturals and encourage them. In my experience, about one in ten of the people you hire will have the potential to rise in the business.

My personal view on managing people is that, on a day-to-day basis, I make sure that they know what is expected of them and what their job is. I'm not really interested in formalizing this into, for example, an appraisal system – apart from with the managers. If you're communicating well with staff and helping them to develop, there should be no real need to sit down with them on an annual basis and go through what their objectives were and how well they achieved them. But later on in the process of selling a business, it may be necessary to put formalities into place such as appraisal systems, job descriptions and personal development plans.

If that time has come in your business, then Item 7 in the Entrepreneur's Toolkit, The formal documentation of staff appraisal, might come in handy. It's about just such systems.

DELEGATE, DON'T ABDICATE

One further point about people is the topic of delegation. There's too much in a growing business for one person to do it all, so you have to delegate. But maybe another difference between the entrepreneur and the business manager is that while entrepreneurs may delegate responsibility, they never abdicate responsibility. Never assume that a delegated task will happen just as you want. Always keep an eye on all aspects of your business and make adjustments where necessary.

Having said that, I do believe in making sure that the person to whom you have delegated should know precisely what's expected of them. Play it by ear and see it from their point of view. Some people are quite comfortable with a casual discussion about what needs to be done. Others, particularly if they've come to you from a big company with heavy human resources processes in place, will be happier with a more formal discussion and documentation of the objectives you want them to achieve. Everyone's different, so you need to adjust the way you manage them to suit their style, motivate them and give them the best possible chance to succeed.

I take a much more hands-on style during difficult times, however. If you delegate, people make mistakes. You can handle errors when times are good, but they can be literally fatal when recession bites. So I look in detail at things like menus and purchases in a way that I would probably delegate outside a downturn.

CHANGING GEAR

The biggest challenge we faced during this growth period was to bid in an open tender to develop a site under the promenade at the beach in Brighton. There are a series of brick arches on the beach that support the promenade. For the previous few years they had been leased from Brighton Corporation by a sailing club and acted as boat sheds. The sailing club had taken the single large space and bricked it up into several smaller units.

This was a big deal, since it was part of the strategic plan of the local authority to build the new image of Brighton as a vibrant and up-to-date tourist resort. Brighton was taking this redevelopment very seriously. Many people see the town as an extension of London and they expect the same standards and sophistication from the leisure facilities. And when local authorities are hell-bent on achieving something, there are opportunities galore for entrepreneurs to get their share of the action. This is particularly true during a recession when a local authority's options are more limited

PAPER TALK

Always look for opportunities; if there's a bandwagon, make sure that you're on it.

A World Cup is an entrepreneur's dream. It works on so many levels. The big boys with their corporate millions are hoping for their pay-off. The sports retailing chains have container-loads of authentic replica shirts fresh from the South China Sea. The brewers have been gearing up for the half-time lager binge for months. Even B&Q reports record sales of barbecues. And butchers across the land are struggling to satisfy our appetite for all things meaty at sizzling sporting gatherings. Look for your angle on a big sporting occasion or an Olympics. People make money out of them.

We knew that if we were to win such a tender, we would have to do it against some big guns: large companies with an impressive ability to use their own architects and other professionals to draw up plans that were bound to impress the good councillors and local authority officials; and that's not to mention their entertainment budget for the same group of people.

To run your own business needs you to be bullish, always taking an optimistic view of how things will turn out. In order to make the fastest progress possible, you also have to be prepared to take a few risks with, for example, the authorities. Suppose you have bought the lease of a café/bar in a town centre that just cries out for tables and chairs on the pavement outside it. Technically you need planning permission to do this. But planning permission takes time, and your potential customers are looking for a drink in the open air right now. It's got to be very tempting to pre-empt the planning permission and just put the tables and chairs outside straight away. Faced with a slightly naughty decision such as this, what I do is ask myself: 'What is the most likely outcome and what is the worst thing that could happen if it goes wrong?' In this case, the worst thing that could happen is that the local authority notices what you are doing or has it brought to their attention. It then tells you to stop doing it. You apologise profusely, remove the tables and chairs and make a planning application immediately. Apologise again on the application form for acting prematurely, but also point out that while the tables and chairs were on the pavement you did not get one complaint. Nevertheless, be very careful: you've got to get on with the authorities and if you upset them badly they can make life difficult.

This project made us realize that we had to change the presentation of the business if we were to form a close relationship with the local authority – our putative landlords. We had to raise our game. For a start, we increased our level of professionalism and set aside enough money to do the job well. We hired professional architects to do the drawings. We employed a major marketing research organization to put credibility behind our gut feel of what the project should include. And we listened and listened to councillors and officials as they gave their views about what the area should look like. Along with about 30 other organizations we put in our business plan to the council – and we won.

I believe that the main reason we won was because our plan best fitted the council's seafront development plan. We had worked out accurately what it wanted and come up with a variety of uses: café, bar, comedy areas, places for bands and musicians to give concerts and so on. We had adapted our original thoughts to bring them more into line with the council's. We came up with a multi-use venue that could be a restaurant, bar and performance space. We knew that would tick all the boxes, and it did.

Maybe the whole business of entrepreneurship comes down to little more than the ability to see things from other people's points of view. See it from the customers' point of view, the suppliers' point of view, your staff's and anyone else's who can have an impact on the success of the business. When people are presented with an idea or a set of facts, they instantly start to think, 'What's in it for me?' If you can anticipate this and realize how they can benefit from a proposal you're making, then you're seeing it from their point of view and you're much more likely to get the result you want.

So, the local authority offered us the lease of the premises, but we still had to get a licence for the sale of alcohol. This is an entirely separate process from, for example, getting planning consent. The way it's done has been changed, but at that time basically you went in front of a magistrate in court and offered evidence to prove that there is a need for licensed premises. If the magistrate believes there is a need, he or she will grant the licence; if not, you get a refusal.

I did the presentation myself and to begin with, it looked as though it had gone very well. The magistrate was complimentary about our plan and agreed that there was a need for an entertainment centre in that area, since young people needed somewhere to let off steam and the beach was a place that would have the least effect on the rest of the population in terms of noise and disturbance. He didn't, however, see the need for alcohol. He believed, I suppose, that young people searching for somewhere to spend their Friday and Saturday nights would choose cafés, bars and clubs where they could chat, dance, listen to a band or a stand-up and generally let their hair down with the occasional break for a coke or a cup of tea with, perhaps, a slice of cake. Yep, that would have them flocking in.

What had gone wrong? Well, there was a company in Brighton which used the brand name Zap. It had outlets for various products and services. It was involved in street theatre and other artistic events. Some people referred to them as 'the luvvies of Brighton'. Its owners were well-known establishment people, well connected to the great and good of the town. They ran the pretty famous Zap Club, a night-club whose premises happened to be next to the arches site that was the subject of our application. The Zap Club objected to our application for a liquor licence. The owners said that there were not enough potential customers, that there would be a decline in standards, and that if we were successful, the people who worked at the Zap Club could potentially lose their jobs.

The magistrate agreed with the Zap Club's line of argument and declined our application. Obviously, without the liquor licence our plan ground to a halt. We were well thought of and favourite to develop the site, but we were up against a brick wall.

At the time, some of our advisers and the people around us suggested that it was not worth fighting such an impasse. It's tempting to say that we felt so bad we thought about giving up; but quite honestly I don't remember considering giving up for a moment. We had the best plan, it was a great business opportunity and we were determined to see it through.

There followed a three- or four-month period during which we could appeal to the Crown Court in Lewes. We were reasonably confident that we could paint the magistrate's decision as somewhat perverse. But there was still the problem of the Zap Club's objection and as long as that was on the table there had to be some doubt whether we would win. Being denied the licence would entail losing a lot of money: the money we would now have to spend on the appeal would be added to the money we had already spent in preparing the plan and the legal expenses involved in the original application. We could only think of one cast-iron way of getting the Zap Club to withdraw its objection, so we took it.

We decided to buy the Zap Club. That way we could neutralize the immediate problem of the objection. Also, looking ahead, we realized that we could programme the two venues so that they would complement each other and not compete. We made an offer to buy the Club, including the freehold premises it was currently occupying. To do that, we needed £750,000. This was another occasion where our decision only to take £10,000 a year each out of the business as salary paid huge dividends. There is no way we could have borrowed 100% of the £750,000, but we could, and did, borrow £500,000 from a brewery that knew us and our methods well. The other £250,000 came from our cash in the business. Without that cash, the whole project would probably not have happened. We signed a contract for the freehold venue and withdrew Zap's objection to our liquor licence. We were quietly pleased with ourselves, having turned a major problem into an opportunity. If entrepreneurs continuously search for new opportunities, they start to occur more and more.

Our legal advice was that without that objection, the chances were better that the appeal would succeed. In fact, we took the risk of signing the arches lease just before the case went to court. As expected, the Crown Court judge ruled that if there were, as the magistrate had agreed, a need for the project as described, there must be a need for the alcohol licence as that was a fundamental part of the project, and in any case there were no objections. Job done and the project went ahead.

BRANCHING OUT AND PREPARING TO EXIT

Even if you think your business may be worth a million pounds, it's not the time to rest on your laurels. During this chapter I'll cover:

- Expanding your product set to take advantage of your market knowledge
- Thinking about new products and new markets
- Setting a long-term or exit strategy
- Branding your business to increase its value

EXPANDING THE PRODUCT RANGE

Making the arches premises work and opening a restaurant helped us realize what our strengths were and what our marketing strategy should be. The restaurant was called Cactus Canteen and we learnt a lot from opening it, not just by gaining experience but also from the people we brought in to run it. We hired an experienced restaurant manager who taught us a lot about the art of running a restaurant, especially the huge difference between a restaurant and a pub that serves food. We also brought in a top-notch chef.

Our biggest knowledge asset was our customer base. We were really well tuned into students and young people who had recently started work and therefore recently started to have real money. If we could sell them beer and shots in a bar they liked, what else could we encourage them to buy?

We exploited this customer base in a number of ways that were related to each other. Such a customer base listens to the radio; so we helped to set up a radio station and got a 20% stake in it. This allowed us to use our influence to get the advertising right for our customer base at a very good cost. The station played the sort of music our customers liked. Young people were choosing to exercise in gyms, so we started up a fitness club from scratch. So quite quickly, a young person in Brighton could go for a drink after work in one of our bars. They could have an evening meal in a bar or restaurant. They could buy a condom in case they got lucky and move on to a club. In the morning, feeling perhaps a little fuzzy, they could clear their heads by doing some weight training and using a treadmill in our gym. While jogging on the treadmill they could listen to local radio playing their sort of music. They could then choose the Cactus Canteen restaurant they'd heard about from the radio station for a hot and spicy lunch. And they could do all of that without leaving premises and venues owned and run by Simon and me. The business schools call this vertical marketing; we just called it knowing a market segment extremely well, keeping up to date with it by listening to customers and encouraging feedback, and then deciding what else we could sell them.

I think it's worth taking a moment to go over the risks involved in introducing new products and attacking new markets as you grow your business. There are, of course, three possibilities:

- Take a new product to an existing market.
- Take an old product to a new market.
- Take a new product to a new market.

Let's look at the implications of these three concepts.

You can see that what we mainly did was to take a new product into an existing market of customers that we knew and who knew us. This is by far the least risky way to go. After all, you've got the feedback from your existing customers giving you on-the-spot advice for what they like and want. The key to this approach to expanding your business is to make sure that you have the skills that will ensure the new products meet the market's expectations and give customer satisfaction. Buy the skills in if you don't have them; remember that by this stage, you're past being a business manager and have become an entrepreneur. You're trying to make money out of other people's work, not just your own.

If, for example, yours is a premises-based business, make sure you're making every corner of the property work for you. I think it's a crime to have unused space. If you rent out unused space to another enterprise, this can be a useful contribution to paying your fixed costs. This is particularly true if the new product is aimed at your market; it's another reason for your target market to come into your premises, even if in the first place it's just to walk through to get to the new service. A very good example of this was a men's grooming product shop. The owners rented out space to masseuses and other grooming-treatment providers. You can even share the risk with the sub-lessee by agreeing a deal that shares their profits rather than agree a fixed rent. If they're successful you make more than the rent money.

Taking your existing products into a new market is rather riskier and hard work. You have to go through the market research side again, so you're essentially starting from scratch. And, of course, there are people trying to kill your entry into the new market as quickly as they can. These people are the competition – they are already supplying the market. A restaurant I worked with hit just such a problem.

It was selling upmarket food at quite high prices. Its entry into the market damaged the business of the pub across the road. The owners of the pub, of course, did not take the intrusion lying down. They hired a new chef, got some local publicity for him and set the price of a three-course meal at the same level as a main course in the restaurant. Another example of competitive behaviour concerns a business consultant I know, who tried to take his training materials into a new industry. He alarmed the two big consultancies, who were already doing a lot of work in the industry, by winning a big contract against their competition. They put a lot of resources into emphasizing to their clients how well they knew the industry and supplying them with industry-specific reports and research findings. They didn't stop his entry into their market entirely, but they certainly kept him away from of a number of plum customers.

Finally there's the big one: taking a new product into a new market that you haven't addressed before – very difficult because you're learning about both sides of the business as you go along. On the product side you'll probably get it a bit wrong to begin with, perhaps having to spend too much to achieve customer satisfaction. On the market side you've got all the hazards of getting your research right and finding a route to promote your product to the market. The competition knows how to get the product right and how to adjust it as the market changes its needs and wants. And, as I've said many times before, they have the huge advantage of knowing the market from the real experience of selling to it and listening to the customer feedback. This may all seem a bit academic, but this new product to a new market is exactly what every entrepreneur starting their first business is doing. It's another way of pointing out the high level of risk you have to take. We allayed this risk by choosing a market that we knew quite well because we were members of it ourselves.

We'll come back to this topic when we get to branding.

SUGGESTION BOX

It's never too early to think about expanding your product range. Sit down and think about related products to yours that you could take – either directly or through other people – to the market you're aiming at with your first idea. You don't have to create a spreadsheet and work out the return to five decimal places; you just need to have the vision to see where you could go next. Doing this at an early stage may also change the way you implement your original idea. Perhaps by doing some fine-tuning you could signal to the market how else you might be able to serve them beyond your initial presentation. If you really think that your first idea is all you can or want to take to the market, you might have to consider whether the idea will support you in making a living but not support you in making a million. It's another angle on the expandability attribute of a good business idea.

Our company was now growing like anything. Indeed, we were in the Sunday Times Fast Track 100, a league for British enterprises that ranks the top 100 by their increase in turnover over the previous 12 months. We were number 78 in the list, growing by about 75% a year. We had grown from £1 million turnover to £5.2 million in just three years. It's an interesting league, because you don't apply to join it; the researchers come and find you.

By this time we were thinking hard about how to add value to the business, with the ultimate (but fairly vague) aim of selling up at some point. It seemed to us that the way to go was to build a brand similar to something like Coffee Republic. We also thought that the way to go was to expand the business and show that it was much bigger than the sum of Martin Webb and Simon Kirby. We changed the name of the holding company from Webb Kirby Ltd to C-Side Ltd and started up two new pubs branded with the name 'Polar Bar'.

We decided on Polar Bar because we saw the big guys developing brands such as All Bar One and Slug and Lettuce. We knew that the sort of investor that comes from the city would add value to a company that had an emergent brand in its portfolio. The Polar Bar logo was based on those frosty designs you see on the door of freezer compartments, a reminder of something that everyone has seen many, many times. We used all the interior design cues of the day: mosaics, stainless steel and a real mishmash of furniture. The music was club based, with live DJs at weekends. It worked enormously well. Simon and I opened two outlets and our successors another two.

As you might expect, the course we steered for our business was not all plain sailing. We made one notable mistake when the business was going pretty well. By then we had already reached a stage where the mistake wasn't a big one; it was more of a blip really. We could ride out such a blip because we'd built up the business to a certain size, but it still took money and a certain amount of stress to sort it out. Anyway, it's an interesting story because it illustrates the point that if your current strategy is working, you should stick with it.

We bought a pub called the Richmond. It was a live rock music pub and you paid to go in. A man who was a huge fan of heavy rock and indie music had started it up to attract the sort of customer who wanted that kind of music. This was a departure for us, since our other venues kept to music from the club scene.

It was all a bit of a shock. When I went into any of our other outlets I was used to being greeted by one or more customers, basically as a pal. I spent time talking to them and listening to them because that was how I kept my ear to the ground for what they liked and what might be the next craze. The customers in the Richmond were a completely different kettle of fish and they simply didn't like us. They saw us as quasi-suits who were running a corporation; if I'm honest, we didn't like them much either. Looking back, the mistake had two aspects: the first was that we were venturing outside our known and understood customer base; the second was that we had stumbled into a business that served a very specialized market that we just didn't understand. Why did we not spot what would happen? A touch of arrogance perhaps; it was the first time we had taken over a bar and failed to grow it fast by making it very busy. I really cannot emphasize enough the truth of the mantra, 'Stick to the markets you know'. Anyway, we paid for the mistake by losing £30,000 during the ten months we ran it. In fact we'd got the lease for nothing, so when we sold it we actually made on the deal.

SETTING A LONG-TERM STRATEGY – OUR FOUR-PRONGED ATTACK

Come exit time, we had decided on the long-term strategy, which was to sell the business. We identified a number of areas that needed work were we to attract one or more potential buyers:

- Continued focus on the Polar Bar brand.
- Publicity for the C-Side company.
- Continued development of the management team.
- Getting the business into a highly organized state so that we could leap the various legal and financial hurdles of making the sale.

Continued focus on the Polar Bar brand

To create a series of outlets, you need to create a brand, with a name that people can identify. Here are some points on branding and some tips on the best time to sell all or part of the brand you're creating. A branded outlet presents an environment where people know what to expect. You can do this with a website as well as with premises.

The brand represents a type and level of service that people can anticipate and rely on.

Start by thinking about the right name. If you choose to buy an existing outlet, perhaps not a very successful one, and stay in the same business, it's probably best to change the name immediately. If the business is reasonably successful, don't change the name too quickly or you may lose the current customer base.

We can learn from big business here. If a major player wants to go into a new market with a new product, they never assume that the brand name that works well for existing products will do just as well for the new ones. An 'upscale' (to use the American term) or 'posh' (to use the British) car was not on Ford's price list for many years. When the company decided to sell a luxury range, it realized that the Ford name would not sell well to that market. So instead of building its own new car, which it could certainly have done, it preferred to buy other marques such as Jaguar and Range Rover. If the target market for your first outlet is similar to the existing market, there may be no need to change the name immediately. Indeed, that may be a mistake.

If you're growing by acquisition and buy another brand smaller than yours, be very careful again not to change the name too quickly. First of all, you need to get the local interpretation of your brand established without frightening existing customers away; then when you're bringing in new customers it may be time to stamp the group's brand name on the new outlets.

The key to the right name is that it gives a clear impression of the feel of the place you're being invited to patronise, or is fairly neutral with a tinge of the type of people you think your outlet will attract.

I talked to two people who were considering the word 'Koncept' for their salon selling men's grooming and treatments. I tried hard to understand why. Why does just changing the first letter of the word 'Concept' give a satisfactory name? Their explanation, that they were trying to sell a new concept and that changing the first letter would make it different and more memorable, wasn't terribly convincing.

I believe their thoughts on this at the beginning of their dream project were too biased towards a slogan rather than a business plan. When I asked them what their objectives were they replied, 'We want to challenge the concept of male grooming and change how people live. When you buy from us, you're not buying a grooming product; you're buying a lifestyle.' Hmm, you see what I mean about a slogan rather than a strategy?

They talked a lot about customer service, but again, I couldn't accept that their customer service would be better than some very good competitive outlets I'd seen. As I've often said, good customer service means that you're playing for a draw with your competitors.

Pushed on why anyone would choose their shop rather than anyone else's, for example Boots, they eventually made some very good points. They're experienced salespeople who know how to ask customers questions to establish what they need. They're experts in the products themselves – they know what products are suitable for different sorts of skins, oily or not, and so on. People would come to them for their knowledge.

Here were skills that offered a genuine competitive edge. They needed to realize this so that their plan for how they would deal with their customers and build their brand was based on these skills. This was good stuff, and if they allowed that thinking more into the front of their minds and left slogans to people on white chargers, they'd find a better name and have a heightened chance of growing the business. Maybe then they could worry about changing the world for men's grooming into a better place.

Another thing that really struck me was when one of them said, 'We'd rather spend ten minutes selling someone the right product than five minutes selling them a more expensive product that wasn't exactly right.' Mmm. Well, if they're talking about a tourist who's not going to be in London for a long time, I can't help thinking that their plan would be better to go for the shorter time and the more expensive product. Having said that, when people are drawing in their spending horns, their approach may be more appropriate.

There's a hairdressing chain that's been very successful called Haringtons. The two original founders have created their dream: a chain of salons in the south of England, now growing by acquisition. I love their starting point; so let's talk about that and come back to the name.

The founders were trained and had worked in London. Young hairdressers with big ideas, they met working locally in the Thames Valley and had the idea that bringing a taste of London to the suburbs could catch on. 'We wanted to offer a London salon experience out of town,' commented Robert Smith, joint director of the Haringtons group. 'We had worked in London and saw a definite need locally for a salon that could offer clients the most current styles and colours, in an amazing salon environment, with caring service by professional staff.' Yep, I can see what they're trying to sell and whom they're trying to sell it to.

I also like the fact that they're repeating something that's worked somewhere else. My view is that it's wrong to be too fashionable or too trendy. The market gets narrower. Don't go for the bottom of the market either: it's too price sensitive. We've talked in technology terms about being leading edge rather than bleeding edge. By bleeding edge I mean taking on the teething troubles and risks of very new technology. By this definition, ultra trendy in retailing terms can be bleeding edge.

Haringtons believed that its success came from putting clear procedures in place from the start and devising a strong education programme; its owners reckoned that having skilled and happy staff was one of their main priorities, again right from the start. This is my experience too.

So, back to the name Haringtons. It's fairly neutral but has a touch of class about it, and all their brochures and business cards and so on use the word 'hairdressing' to explain what they're for. You will, of course, notice that despite what I've said about Koncept, Haringtons has changed one letter in the more normal spelling of Harrington. This reminds us that selecting a brand name is a very personal business. A picture that someone puts on the wall may do a lot for them and nothing for me, and vice versa. You have to make decisions and, in the end, take your own risks.

One more quick point on names – some people believe that your business name should have the echo of an existing branding or positioning. It should almost suggest that new customers have heard of you before. The Brook Gallery has absolutely nothing to do with the Brook Street employment agency and is a brilliant example of this. It's not passing off, which is illegal, but making sure that the associations people have with the name are positive and relevant. As another example, there's a hairdressing salon in Maidenhead, where Haringtons started, called 'Headingtons'.

Branding experts talk in these or similar terms: they talk about the 'weight' of the brand, how dominant the brand is in its market place. This is not just market share, it is influence, and the ability of the brand to survive new competition. They talk then of the timescale of the brand, how long it has been established. The longer the better in terms of survival and growth in the brand's geographic reach. They then look at breadth, how wide the age spread is, how many types of consumer the brand attracts, how geographically spread it can become and the spread of different products or services that can use the brand name.

I admit that this looks like the sort of exercise the marketing companies of large brands like Gillette and Disney might spend a lot of time with, but it does have some uses for the budding entrepreneur. You can look at the brands you're competing with in those terms. How will you differentiate from the big brands, for example?

You can also use it for planning purposes, asking yourself: Where could we expand geographically that does not carry a huge risk? What other services might we offer from the same branded premises? It's quite useful to think from time to time in this way; it emphasizes that the real return will come if your business becomes a recognized and respected brand.

One of the big advantages of branding for us was that our spend on advertising was more effective since we were promoting five bars with the same name. We could, for example, afford a decent radio campaign.

This has a huge impact on the putative value of your business. It is an inescapable fact that when investors set up a new business they are taking a considerable risk. The money spent in setting the premises up will probably represent a fair whack of the first few months' gross takings. There is no certainty that the product will sell or that it will sell in that location.

The risk then diminishes as you reach and pass the monthly break-even point on a regular basis. Then maybe the time has come to move into the next phase of growth. This time the risk is a good bit less. It's like my experience of do-it-yourself. I don't really believe in it because what happens is that you do everything once. You never have a chance to learn from your inevitable mistakes and then do the job again, this time much better. That is the difference between the amateur and the professional: the professional learns from experience and repeating the same procedures time and time again.

So the risk is a good bit less with the second outlet. After the third business set-up you've reduced the really savage risk of losing all the investors' money to pretty small, unless you really are in, for example, the fashion business. Now think about what you've got to sell. To begin with you had nothing but your passion and your dedication, backed up with the promise of working very hard. In such circumstances an investor is going to ask for a reasonably big share of your business as a carrot for taking the risk.

The situation has changed after, say, the third outlet. You have a track record, your skills are much sharper and you've dealt with all your weaknesses by training or by using the skills of other people. You might even have a brand. Investors are going to have to pay a lot more for your business in this more advanced state.

If the founding investors, perhaps including you, were looking for a pretty quick exit strategy for a good return on their investment, this could actually be the right time to sell some or all of their shares to someone paying a premium for the potential of the brand. Or they could stick around.

I raise this situation because I quite often see businesses that get to this lower-risk stage of development and start to dream about the brand really taking off and becoming an international chain to rival McDonald's and Starbucks. They then take the business into the next phase – perhaps a diversification of product or a venture into another part of the country or another part of the world. In risk terms, they're about to go into another situation where they don't have that much experience and may be unaware of some of the pitfalls, or the new skills they're going to need. The risk has increased again.

My point is that, as always, it's a balance. Do you want to stay in with your entire holding or reduce your overall return by taking some now and potentially losing out on further and bigger returns later on? The cardinal rule is that the value of a business is much higher when it has demonstrated success with a brand in a business that can grow organically than when it's venturing into new areas. Obviously, you don't want to own a very small percentage of the shares when it really goes mad because you've sold a large stake to another investor, but 'a bird in the hand' and all that might be worth having. Don't forget that if you've sold your business quite early you can always start over again, this time with your own money and with a nice, low-risk profile.

You need to step back from time to time and look at the risks you are taking, because at times they go higher rather than lower.

You mustn't mistime the selling of the business either. Two guys set up a publishing company with a difference. They built a massive base of intellectual property by publishing paperbacks and selling them through the book trade to consumers – a pretty standard way of operating. The brand became successful quite quickly because they had the right skills and a lot of experience in this area.

The second part of the plan was to sell the rights to their intellectual property to companies in tailored, paperback or electronic form. This was a venture that had been tried in a number of ways by other publishers, but not quite in this fashion and not terribly successfully.

They got their first two small corporate deals and then had the dilemma – do we sell part of the business now with all its potential or do we stick it out? I think they needed to go over the risk/value relationship of the business they were building. They might have wanted to stick it out and achieve immortality with their own self-built brand or they might just have wanted to take advantage of their profile at that time. It was worth less then, but it might have been a good time to sell because of its massive potential for future profits.

The truth is that they missed the high season for selling businesses before the recession. They could still sell the business or parts of it, but they would get less for it because there are fewer people with money to invest. Buying and selling businesses goes out of fashion in a downturn. When people are pouring money into buying up businesses, don't miss the boat.

What is the principal reason that individuals tend not to make a lot of money on the stock exchange? Is it that they buy the wrong stocks? Not necessarily; if you buy enough to make a balanced portfolio of stocks you should do pretty much as well as the 'experts'. No, the main reason is that they don't sell at the right time. They think that a rising market will never stop, and accept very dubious explanations of why circumstances have changed and that the market will indeed keep rising for the foreseeable future. Then the crash or downturn comes and they're lucky to get out with their original stake. I have a grave suspicion that there's a lesson in there for someone building a business or a brand.

Publicity for the C-Side company

We mounted a big PR and publicity campaign. For example, we put banners outside every site promoting the C-Side name. Since we had 30 sites, people started to realize how big we had become and how much we were part of the Brighton scene, let alone the employment scene – we then had 350 people working for us. As luck would have it, the Labour Party conference came to Brighton that year and we put out banners saying 'C-Side Welcomes New Labour'. I stirred up all my contacts in the local press and radio and got the banners into the papers. This campaign really did create a great awareness that all the sites were owned by the same company and a realization that, with banners all over the place, the business community should start to take us more seriously as a company of some substance.

The continued development of the management team and the staff

By this time there were three key managers in the business besides Simon and me. They were Nik Downs, operations; Giles Beal, our accountant; and Kate Johnson in the marketing role. All three were hugely important in running and growing the business, and they were pretty special people. Giles, for example, is one of the most unlikely accountants you'll ever meet. He was a surfer who was out in the pubs and clubs three or four times a week. This made him understand the market completely and as a result made the figures come alive to him, so his contribution to discussions was much more than a simple rehearsal of the figures. Nik was our product expert. He was a great barman and mixed a mean cocktail. He had huge energy and a love of the industry and he channelled that energy into delighting our customers. Kate started out as a part-time member of our bar staff. She was one of those people who immediately caught our eye: she was full of energy, feisty and held strong opinions. Great with customers, she was bursting with good ideas and enthusiasm. After she got some further experience working for a festival-organizing company, we threw her in at the deep end as marketing manager. Kate took charge of posters, ads and flyers and she thrived. What's her big secret? Well, guess what? She really understood our customer base. Kate carried on as marketing director after we sold the business and now runs a successful design and print business on the web.

We recognized these people's contribution by paying them decent salaries, giving them company cars and bonuses and, of course, keeping them – and the other people who worked for us – involved in the partying culture that was a hallmark of the company and of staff relations. We held lots of parties and always endeavoured to make working for the company great fun, both during and after work. Even though we now had 350 people, I made sure I knew most of them by name and they certainly knew me – I still spent a lot of time in each bar getting feedback from the staff as well as customers. As I've mentioned before, the bar business is notorious for 'shrinkage', the polite term for people stealing stock or fiddling the tills. In my experience, people are much less likely to steal from the owners of a business if they know them well and meet them frequently, than they are from a large anonymous corporation.

Making the business highly saleable

It's simple common sense to think about getting the business to look as attractive as possible. When you sell a company, the buyers go through a process known as 'due diligence'. It's a method by which a purchaser or an investor in a business investigates the records of the target company to make sure that they support the alleged value of the business, and to discover if there are any skeletons in the cupboard. It's a process that happens once you have concluded initial sales terms, including the price to be paid, and holds dangers for a selling company that is ill-prepared for the process. The problems are threefold.

1 If the records do not entirely support the current owners' claims for the business, the potential purchaser may well drop the value of their bid.
2 If the buyer finds things they were not expecting, they can start to doubt the integrity of the sellers and may well pull out of the deal.

3 If there are any anomalies, it is bound to cause delay to the purchasing process.

So that we could leap the various legal and financial hurdles of making
the sale, we looked at all the items that would be involved in the
process of due diligence so that when it was time for a potential buyer
to go through the process, they would be able to do it quickly and
without any major glitches.

Due diligence is likely to cover:

- the past and forecast financial performance of the business
- the accounts and methods of accounting
- valuation of property and other assets
- compliance with legal and tax regulations
- any outstanding legal actions against the business
- major customer contracts
- protection of patents and other forms of intellectual property

In our case, preparing for due diligence included a close look at the
leases of all our premises and tidying up any loose ends. Indeed, in
a couple of cases where the leases had little time to run, we negotiated new leases. We also negotiated as many rent reviews as we could,
asking landlords to bring the review forward where that was appropriate. We got rid of any odd clause or covenant that might hinder a
sale. We got up to date with all the staff contracts, and made sure
the Health and Safety manuals were current and complete. Basically,
we focused on the administrative areas of the business – the bits that
tend to get left behind by busy entrepreneurs. Effectively we were
doing due diligence as though we were a buyer, and it paid huge
dividends when we actually found a purchaser. Besides Simon and
myself, we needed – and got – huge cooperation from the three key

people: Nik, Giles and Kate. If due diligence goes well, it makes the whole complicated and difficult process of selling a business that much more certain.

Simon always insists on two key things to make a business more saleable. First of all, he believes that all your dealings should be whiter than white. You should pay your taxes and take seriously all the regulations you have to abide by. If you don't, he thinks that you'll get found out by the buyer and either lose the sale or get a lower price than you could have.

Right, just before I finish the tale of C-Side and what I learnt from it, I think I'll pass on one more quick rant about how we stifle entrepreneurship. If you've got to the rapid growth stage of your business, well done! In fact, double well done – because you've probably got where you are now by swimming against the establishment tide.

PAPER TALK

I heard a sad tale on the *Today* programme recently. A bright 13-year-old boy had taken it upon himself to make some extra pocket money. Urged on by his father, who promised to quit smoking if he made a profit, the lad started selling sweets and soft drinks to his classmates. He bought multi-packs from Asda, broke them up and sold the single units to his pals for a few pence profit. A future Branson was in the making and everyone was happy.

Everyone except the school, that is. They'd come under the influence of Jamie Oliver and his mission to ban all the things that kids like eating (unless they come from Sainsbury's, presumably). In their zeal to make sure their charges ate only raw vegetables, they banned our plucky junior entrepreneur from selling his sugary wares and threatened him with exclusion.

Apart from the fact that everyone of my generation grew up on a diet of sweets, fish fingers, chips and beans and were largely unscathed by the experience, what message does this send out to our budding business brains?

Not a positive one. It's taught this poor boy that his teachers would prefer he learnt from them by sticking to a rigid, fixed curriculum rather than experimenting on his own. His fledgling business would have taught him mathematics, negotiation and much more. All more relevant and useful than the decline of the Aztec empire or whatever schools consider important this week.

CASHING IN

Making your first million has to mean having at least a million in cash. There are lots of senior citizens out there who are millionaires – mainly because of the value of their property – but, ironically, many of them don't have any money. So to me, the million has to be in the bank.

This means that you've got to sell all or part of your business. I prefer all, because I don't really like co-ownership, particularly with City-type gents who you will never get to know or, frankly, trust.

So we had reached the time when we felt ready to put the company on the market. You need specialist help with this, otherwise you won't find a buyer or you'll get a lousy price. We invited a number of accountancy firms specializing in finding buyers for small- and medium-size businesses and ended up with the medium-sized Mazars. This is a nationwide company but we dealt with its Brighton branch. We chose Mazars because the chemistry was good between the two sides and we had some empathy over the size of both companies. We knew that our deal was a major one for the firm and felt that it was big enough to be able to reach a lot of prospective buyers, but small enough for success with our job to be very significant to it. From start to finish, the process took a year.

Mazars set the value. It took the profits of £2.35 million and predicted a multiple of 6.5. We had several offers before the one we accepted. The Foreign and Colonial Venture Capital Company offered us £13.5 million for the company, but that sum bought it cash and debt free. There was net cash in the business that Simon and I were able to take with us. This made the estimated multiple about right.

Interestingly, at no point did the bidders ask Simon or me to stay with the company. We had expected them to insist that we continued to manage the business for a period or even that we should get some of the proceeds from the sale as an earn-out (an earn-out means that the full sum of the offer is only paid when the previous owners of the business have produced the profits they had forecast for two or three years ahead).

Looking back, this was probably a mistake on their part. Here's what they did and why I think they did it. They headhunted a man who had not run a business such as ours before. In fact his background was running a bowling alley. To use a political term, they 'parachuted him in' and imposed him on the management team and the bar managers. He didn't click with the managers and within months we were hearing tales of problems. After six months he still didn't know where all the sites were. We know this because he ordered a taxi to go from one site to another that happened to be two doors down. People were complaining that there was no clear direction and that they did not have specific objectives. He was also only part time, running his own business at the same time; so the three people in the management team, at that time in their 20s, were for the most part just left to get on with it.

Then the new owners extended geographically into Southampton and Bournemouth, which might have been OK if they had recognized the big change of culture in doing that. The people in the business were used to working in a tightly knit group who saw a lot of each other. You can't keep that up if you are too geographically spread.

The new bars got into problems and the three managers spent too much time with the new bars trying to get them to perform. This inevitably meant that the bars in Brighton started to go down. In the event, the three main managers stayed for only a couple of years. It's interesting that Kate and Nik work with me in another business and Giles went to New Zealand. At the time of writing, C-Side now has left only 6 of the 30 sites we sold.

What can we learn from this sad saga? I think it's a good example of someone who wasn't passionate about running the company. You've got to have a passion for the business itself, like Nik, Giles and Kate had, or a passion for growing the business you own. The new manager was not the owner, so he didn't have that type of passion, and he displayed little enthusiasm for the business itself. I mean, part time? What on earth did they think Simon and I did? I also think that venture capital companies are better at going into business and then selling them on than they are at running going concerns.

We were frankly very disappointed by the contraction of the business. I've talked often in this book about the passion that entrepreneurs need to bring to their 'babies'. We had worked so hard to build the business up, and it was awful to see it neglected and deteriorating. On the other hand, though, I've got to be honest, it's made me realize that Simon and I had indeed brought something special to the mix, and that went missing when we left.

So that's it – the history of C-Side and what we learnt from this marvellous experience. I hope that I've been able to pass on some of the lessons that building the business taught us, and that you feel better equipped to have a go yourself. You can do it. I know that from my contacts with so many people who have decided later in life that they missed the opportunity to go it themselves when they were younger, but do take the task on and succeed.

The Entrepreneur's Toolkit that follows should act as a reference for good business practice that might help you through some difficult bits as you build your business. Because, believe me, there will be difficult times. No entrepreneur has made a million without a few sleepless nights and a number of big challenges. But try to see that as a benefit rather than a problem – when you've overcome the problems and made your first million, you'll feel even better than if it had been all plain sailing.

I'm not going to say good luck because, although I know that luck will play some part in your progress, I also know that you make your own luck. No, I'm going to wish you good hunting – just go for it!

THE ENTREPRENEUR'S TOOLKIT

INTRODUCTION

No matter what business you're going into, you've got to keep one eye on the business itself – whether you're satisfying your customers, whether your staff are motivated and operating well – and another eye on the financial implications of what you're doing. So, whether your dream is a restaurant, a hairdressing salon, an art gallery or a print shop, you've got to master the rudiments of business and business finance if you're going to give yourself a chance of managing the business well. I was frankly rather surprised to find that some of the start-up entrepreneurs I've dealt with didn't even know how to add VAT to an invoice or subtract it from an invoice that included VAT. This toolkit incorporates all I think you need to know about finance and some other issues to keep a firm control on your business, presented in what I hope you will find a practical and useable way.

Contents

1 The general business model and working capital
2 Risk assessment
3 Getting the start-up money
4 Drawing up the first rough financial plan
5 The decision to lease premises or buy them
6 Drawing up a detailed business plan
7 The formal documentation of staff appraisal

1   THE GENERAL BUSINESS MODEL AND WORKING CAPITAL

Let's have a look at the theory behind what went wrong at the Helsinki. The figure on page 129 is a model of how money travels round a business – in this case a pub. At the start, the owners of the business put in a certain amount of share capital – in our case a very small amount

THE GENERAL BUSINESS MODEL

of capital. We then borrowed a further £60,000 to get the business started and this went into the company as loan capital. The implications of loan capital are that you have to pay interest at an agreed, regular time, normally monthly. If you don't pay the interest then, of course, the loan amount is increasing and will cost more when you come to the other implication of loan capital – you have to pay the stuff back. You can, of course, put in your own hard-earned cash as loan capital, in which case the business may not have to pay it back.

This capital (1) goes into the bank account as cash (2). In our case we started to spend it, first on fixed assets (3), the furnishings, fittings and cost of the building project. The rest of the cash goes into working capital, where it gets spent to pay back the short-term creditors (4). Creditors in this case are the staff (5); they're only creditors for a week or a month, that is until the next payday. As well as the staff there are other overheads (6) occurring continuously – utility bills, telephone bills, commodities such as cleaning materials and so on. Finally there is stock (7) to buy – in our case beers, wines, spirits and food – this stock we hope will become sales (8), and thus come back into the tills as cash (2).

Now what we learnt to do from the disastrous experience of the Helsinki was to leave this cash in as working capital to fund any problems. When you have worked out the sum of your labour costs and other overheads on, say, a weekly basis, you can decide how much money you want to leave in the business as working capital. Ideally you want to build up two months' worth of labour and overheads as spare working capital or cover, so that you have time to deal with any eventuality. (This is, admittedly, the 'perfect world scenario' and if you're trying to expand a business by, for example, opening another outlet, you probably need to take all the cash you've got to start up the new business and perhaps go overdrawn; but again, that's a calculated risk and not a matter of spend, spend, spend.)

At Helsinki we didn't have any cover; on the contrary, we took the concentrating out of the business as drawings (9) and lived the life of Riley.

What else can we learn from this first outline of the model? Well, if your business deals with other companies, you will probably not be paid in cash. The money due on sales will go into debtors (10) and stay there until the corporations pay up, when it goes back into cash. A lot of the job of a start-up entrepreneur is balancing creditors and debtors to make sure that the working capital stays manageable. Unfortunately, if people take a long time to pay you, you've got to get tough; and don't pay your creditors before you really have to. This gets harder and harder during a recession, since everyone is concentrating on the same thing.

When you have good control of your working capital, you're in a position to garner cash ready for your next enterprise, like expanding by taking on the lease of another property and starting your second outlet.

2   RISK ASSESSMENT

There are two benefits of acknowledging the risks that are bound to go with any business you are about to start. First, you find out if the risks involved do, in fact, outweigh the benefits of starting the business of your dreams. If there is a high probability (i.e. risk) that a big chain in the same business as you is about to start up across the road, for example, that could be a deal breaker. The second reason is that a risk identified and documented is one that you can manage and mitigate. In the same example, you might decide that the risk is worth taking provided you can identify a unique selling proposition for your business that is plainly different from and, at least for the market you are chasing, better than the other chain's offering. It's important to take a cold, hard view on risk. Unrealistic enthusiasm has got lots of people in trouble. Hard as it may be, make sure you listen to people who put your idea down – they may just have something.

By the way, the term unique selling proposition – USP – is a useful one. It is the attribute of your offerings to customers that distinguishes it from all your competitors. It's a useful exercise to think about what exactly your USPs are – both in terms of defining your strategy and also because it will enable you to answer the question when the bank manager asks, 'So, what is the USP of the business you're planning to start?' And they will ask, even if only to demonstrate that they understand the jargon.)

So the purpose of risk analysis is to be realistic in listing the risks and to have a plan for managing the main ones. In the end, this boils down to two questions:

1 Do you and your family agree to accept the lifestyle risks in order to gain the lifestyle benefits?
2 Is the level of risk that comes with setting up the business acceptable?

The basic principles of risk assessment are these:

- All new businesses will carry some risks in terms of successful implementation and the achievement of the desired results. This is true during good times and hard alike.
- You should be proactive in identifying and prioritising risks.
- Where possible, you should take positive action to lower the likelihood that the risk will occur.

- You should plan actions to minimize the effects of the risk if it actually occurs.

Here's a form that you can use to identify and assess the risks of a decision.

RISKS		P	I	ACTION TO MANAGE RISKS	S
A					
B					
C					
D					
E					
F					

The first column is just an identifier for reference purposes. The second highlights the nature of the risk. Ask yourself, 'What are the potential problems associated with this business? What could go wrong?' As a memory jogger or thought starter, you can use these groupings: 'What could go wrong financially?', 'What could go wrong technically?' and 'What could go wrong practically?'. Since the last of these includes those aspects of the business that involve people changing how they do things – your potential customers, for instance – it is likely to be a large area of risk.

The third column marked 'P' is your intuitive feel for how likely it is that the risk will happen. Mark 10 if the chances of occurrence are more or less a certainty, down to 1 where the risk is very unlikely to occur. Some risks have more impact on performance than others. Identify these by marking in the 'I' column the impact that the risk will have on performance or achievement of the decision's objectives. If the impact is low, a marginal impact only, then mark it 1; if the impact is significant, mark it up to 10.

Now look at what could be done to manage the risk. You can look at this in two ways:

- what you can do to minimize the probability that the risk will occur; and
- how you can minimize the impact if it does occur.

Finally, assess the status of each risk, as

1 red – immediate action is required;
2 amber – future action is probably going to be required; or
3 green – there is no action required, either because the probability of its occurring is low or because the impact is low.

When should you perform risk analysis? Obviously before you start the business; but it's also useful when you are about to change something radically, like adding a treatment room to a shop selling grooming products. It's not a bad idea to do it whenever you are planning an activity that could have a significant impact on perform-ance, like thinking about the risk to your first outlet if you start up a second one – will the original outlet continue to do as well as it is at the moment? Once again, the benefit in this last case is that you work out a plan, perhaps for how you split your time between premises, in order to mitigate the possible downturn in the performance of the first outlet.

RISKS		P	I	ACTION TO MANAGE RISKS	S
A	Turnover may be insufficient to take on a full-time treatment room operator	5	6	Make an offer to the person to take on the role as a subcontractor for the first three months	A
B	It may be impossible to serve people quickly enough if we use only fresh produce	6	2	We think we can do it, but if necessary we can use some concentrates in some products	G
C	The German shop fittings we have ordered may be delayed at customs	9	7	Get to know the customs process and speak to someone who could expedite your fittings	R
D					
E					
F					

Those risks with low impact and low probability of occurrence you can more or less forget. For those with a high probability but low impact, you can decide whether or not it's worthwhile trying to prevent the occurrence. Where the impact is high but the probability low, you should look for ways to protect yourself against occurrence and mitigate the impact if they do occur. But the overwhelming focus for action is those risks where the probability is high and so is the impact. This is the case in risk C in the example above: it's vital that you make enquiries straight away to try to avoid a delay to delivery that would then delay the opening of the premises.

The final touch is to mark the risks red, amber or green. Forget the green ones, monitor the amber ones and get cracking on the red ones … NOW.

3 GETTING THE START-UP MONEY

There are various ways of getting the cash you need to start up your business. You may need seed money, for example, to set up your website with the ability to sell directly using secure techniques to protect your customers. If yours is a premises-based business, you will need to pay the deposit on the lease and the first month's rent. If it's not and you're selling on the Internet, you still have start-up costs on your website and warehousing, for example. You may also have to pay a premium if you're leasing a going concern: this is the money that the previous owner of the business can ask for as the goodwill of the current business. You will probably have to pay a premium for the lease, an upfront charge, even if the shop is empty and there is no goodwill. This very much depends on the premises, where you are in the country and the prevailing market conditions. During a recession the market conditions are favourable to buyers, so negotiate hard. You've also got to fit out your new premises and get stocked up. As always, it's crucial to think these issues through and understand the implications of the sources of money, as well as the availability: frequently it's so difficult to find a source of funds that it's tempting to go for the first one that's available, not always with the best results.

Your plan will have as good a budget as you can devise, so you start from knowing how much money you need. You'll get into the detail later; at the moment you need a rough idea so that you can test the water for possible sources of cash.

The two sources of long-term finance in a business are share capital and loan capital. Share capital comes in as your cash, or cash from any other source that buys a share of the business. I am a great believer in saving hard so that you can put in as much money of your own as you can – it's a good discipline, if nothing else. I've always put my own money in as loan capital rather than share capital and had share capital of £100. This means that I can draw the money out of the company as a loan repayment without having to pay tax on it.

You can find other sources of share capital, but make sure you're happy to live with the results of selling part of your company to someone else. A bit like your previous employer, they're trying to make money out of your skills and hard work. Personally I never wanted to give any of my business away and prefer loan capital. However, it may suit you to go this way so that you can find other investors:

- A private source, such as your parents, friends and family. This can be a good source of funds, but does have a downside if things don't go entirely according to plan. Letting down professional investors who understood the risks they were taking is much easier to live with than letting down the family and pals you will continue to deal with after the event. Don't just look to these people as a source of share capital; they can probably help out with a paintbrush too. You don't have to put this money in as share capital. See if you can get them to lend the money for a fixed-interest payment. Remember that when interest rates are very low, people are probably quite right to take a higher risk with their savings than just accepting the very poor return they get from a bank.
- A public source such as a business 'angel'. Angels are professional investors who make small investments in new businesses. The tax

breaks that angels get reduce their risk hugely, and multiply their returns. The upside of this source can include getting the benefit of their advice – because most of them have accumulated their wealth by growing their own businesses. The potential downside is that they will interfere and, if they don't agree with your unfolding strategy, this can be a problem. These people do not entirely disappear during a recession, but it's sure as hell more difficult to find them.

• Venture capital funds. These are professional investors who build up a fund using money from many personal and institutional sources and invest it in a portfolio of start-up and emerging businesses. This has the effect of spreading investors' risk. Mind you, the success rate with venture capital-funded businesses is not high. The fund managers only expect a few in ten to really fly, but they expect to make a princely return on the few that make it. Watch these guys, though: they will try to get a massive amount of your business for as little as they can get away with. The other thing they do is interfere when things are not going according to plan. In fact, they can make matters worse if you are struggling a bit by insisting on getting a consultant's or accountant's report, which, of course, your business has to pay for. They generally avoid investing in completely new businesses; so you might have to get started before you can get them interested.

In one sense, share capital is cheaper than loan capital. In the long run, return on shareholders' capital comes in the shape of dividends that are normally paid out by the company twice a year. But in the early stages of a business, part-owners may very well drop the requirement for dividends and allow you to keep all the profits in the business for expansion. At that stage, the money could be said to be free. Not paying dividends can be tricky, however, because they are a very tax-efficient way of paying the salaries of the owners of the business (dividends do not attract NIC payments, whereas salaries do). If you use this device to pay yourself, you may have to get an agreement that the part-owners of the business waive their share of the dividend.

There is also no necessity for the managers to plan to have the cash to buy the shares back. In practical terms the money is in the company for ever, unlike loan capital that you've eventually got to pay back. There is a cost downside in using external share capital to get a business going: lawyers and accountants (and you can't avoid them) don't come cheap. Oh, and you have to find someone who's happy to take the pretty big risk of putting money into a business that may very well fail, with the consequent loss of their entire capital injection. It's this risk of failure that makes shareholders demand, in the long term, that their overall returns should be higher than those for the providers of loans. They get this return through the growth of cash dividends, which they can take over the long term. Or they look for growth in the capital value of the business and therefore their shares. The capital value of a business is what someone will offer for it and then pay. Venture capitalists want out. That's what they're for – a quick, high risk with a fairly short-term and large return.

Loan capital is probably cheaper to arrange. It comes from banks and financial institutions that measure the risk of the company and then charge an interest rate to reflect that risk.

There is a huge irony here. Time out for a moment to make sure you understand where financial lenders are coming from. If someone offered to lend you £10 for a week, but asked you to agree to pay back twice that amount at the end of the week, you wouldn't need to have read this book to realize that that's a very bad deal. Suppose, however, that you are completely broke and know that you will have £121 benefits payment in cash by the day at which you have to make the capital and 100% interest repayment – still not interested? Ah, I forgot to mention that your two children haven't eaten properly for 36 hours and that they're wailing for food. In such circumstances, the loan sharks of the inner-city sink estates make such loans, and prosper. This is a good starting point for considering the purveyors of loan capital. They're all like that, only the ones in banks are better dressed and less physically threatening. Boy, have they proved all this recently.

Their view is that they tailor their interest charges to protect themselves against the risk of default. The more difficult the situation the borrower is in, the higher the risk and therefore the higher the price of help.

If you are running a huge conglomerate and wish to borrow $250 million to buy up a subsidiary in another country, you will be wined and dined by various moneylenders eager to get your business at, perhaps, less than 1% above the rate at which the banks themselves borrow money. If you need £20,000 to tide your corner shop over a refurbishment, you will probably have to trawl the high street to find a lender willing to lend you the money at 5 or 6% above bank rate. And they will probably want you to back the security of the loan by remortgaging your house or leaving your kids with them as hostages (OK, I made that last bit up). Banks are, indeed, the people who lend umbrellas to small businesses; but only when it isn't raining.

Don't forget that with loan capital, you also have to plan the repayments to keep within the agreed contract when the loan was made. Another irony here – if you have loan capital in your business and even if you're making a reasonable profit, you can still get into trouble when the time comes to find the cash to repay the loan.

One important lesson we learnt from the Helsinki experience was never to confuse turnover with profit. Turnover is what you take at the tills to pay for all your overheads and the direct costs of the products you're selling; profit is the bit that's left over once all the bills are paid and is the bit that belongs to you. Lesson 2 is never to confuse profit with cash. It's quite possible for you to be making a good profit but still not have a viable business. You've taken care of the interest on loans by having it on your overheads list, but you've also got to repay it.

The example below shows a company making a healthy profit. Its return on capital invested at 20% is pretty good. Return on capital employed is what it's all about: it is the number that shows you what return you're getting on your money plus the return you're making on your lenders' money. There is nothing untoward either about the company's ability to pay its interest charges out of its profits. In fact, interest accounts for less than a third of its profits before interest and tax. Here are the numbers:

Long-term debt to bank		60.0
Shareholders' funds – the capital the owners put in		40.0
Capital employed – debt plus shareholders' funds		100.0
Profit before interest and tax		20.0
Return on capital invested		20%
Interest rate	10%	
Interest		6.0
Profit before tax		14.0

Tax rate	25%	
Tax		3.5
Net profit after interest and tax		10.5

OK so far, but unfortunately those numbers only show one of the implications of debt, that is interest. Another one is making repayments. In this case the company has to pay back £12,000 a year on the five-year loan. Now look at the numbers:

Net profit after interest and tax (as before)		10.5
Repayments		12.0
Net cash outflow		−1.5

So, bad luck: the company's making money and running out of cash. It's either going to have to increase its loans or somehow increase its turnover and profit.

Back to bankers – I suppose I've got to be fair to them. I mean, why should they lend you money when you have no track record of running a business? You have to earn the right to have a bank as an interested business partner or money supplier.

Talk to bankers about how to do that. Ask them to paint a picture of what your business would have to look like if they were to help with the next phase of expansion. If you're talking to a banker who has worked with a lot of small businesses, their experience could be very useful. It is actually getting more difficult to find a human being in a bank that you can get to talk to – but persevere, things will get less tight and it's always easier to gain cooperation from people you have spent time talking to.

I am living proof that you can actually start a business using credit from a number of credit cards. I had enough money to buy the lease of a bar and pay the first month's rent. I needed £21,000 to fit it out, decorate it and buy stock. I maxed four credit cards and got the £21K. OK, I know it's expensive if you keep a credit-card loan for a long period of time, but in the short term it's ideal. You've already earned the credit rating from the card providers, so you don't even have to tell them what you're doing. And you don't have to pay much of it back each month. Not only that, but you can get discount interest rates when you first take on the card, then at the end of the discount period change the loan to another provider. It's still quite possible; you just have to be organized enough not to make a mistake in your timing. If you're clever, you can take advantage of free-interest deals by transferring your balances between different cards. Use the free deal and then move on. The banks make enough money out of us, so don't have any qualms about beating them at their own game.

I worked out that, if the cash flow I had planned for actually happened, I could juggle credit cards for a while and then get them paid off in a sensible amount of time, and I didn't want to spend the time and energy persuading someone else to lend it to me when it was already available at the swipe of a card.

Where else can you look? We've talked about remortgaging and it's difficult to avoid this if you have an asset – the house – but no profitable business as yet. So you may have to do it. Finally, shareholders don't give money to everyone, you know; they look for the smart folk. I've done it myself. I have, for instance, very much enjoyed helping a mate to set up a fine arts printing business.

One final point on borrowing – if you're leaving a reasonably well-paid job to go out on your own, make sure you borrow the money before you leave, using the creditworthiness earned by your regular income. Don't tell the lender you're going to give up work and take a huge punt; you'll not only make them nervous – which doesn't matter – but you'll stop them lending you the money as well, which does.

4   DRAWING UP THE FIRST ROUGH FINANCIAL PLAN

The aims of this first draft of the financial plan are as follows:

- to make absolutely sure you understand what the running costs of your business are
- to make sure you know the profit margins of your products
- to understand your break-even point
- to set the foundations of the financial knowledge you will need to run the business and produce the next crucial document – your cash flow
- to set the foundations of your ability to write the financial side of your business plan
- to re-evaluate your whole business proposition and check its financial viability

The importance of break-even analysis and what it does for you

An alarming number of people go into a small business with little or no understanding of the financial side of running a business. I've spoken to one woman who is setting up a company to sell educational materials to childminders. It seems to me that fundamentally it's a good idea and very much of its time. When I suggested she draw up a spreadsheet of her costs and estimated revenues, she replied that she just couldn't get her head around figures and was going to leave all that to the accountant. To be honest, I think that's a bit like driving a car and only seeing road signs every six months. If you can't work these things out, then don't start a business. You'll go bust. It's as simple as that. Get yourself on a course and learn the basics; it'll be money well spent.

I am quite happy for business people to be uncertain how accountants draw up the annual report from the bookkeeping figures, but I'm also convinced that you've got to be able to understand enough about finance to help with two processes. You need to know enough to use the numbers to help with planning, and to read the signals that the numbers give on the state of your business's progress. Properly used, the numbers let you make the fine-tuning adjustments that allow you to go from a mediocre performance to a great one. Of these signals, break-even analysis is by far the most important at the beginning of your dream project.

The difference between success and failure in a new business revolves around how long it takes for the business to start making a profit. While you are still spending more money than you're receiving in sales revenues, you remain uncertain whether your dream is going to come true or turn into a nightmare of sleepless nights.

Here's how it works. Every month you are going to spend money, whether anyone comes through the door to buy something or not. These expenses are called, quite reasonably, fixed costs. They include the rental of the premises, insurances, staff costs, maintenance work, marketing costs and so on. As part of your plan, you need to make an absolutely complete list of these. Don't miss anything out or the calculation will go horribly wrong. Don't forget that you have to pay tax as well and national insurance and VAT; the list is quite lengthy.

Some businesses only have fixed costs. What this means is that no matter how much revenue comes in, they only have the fixed costs to cover before they reach the break-even point. This gives them a very simple break-even analysis.

A transport business is a good example of this. If a bus company runs on a scheduled basis, it uses the same amount of fuel, and suffers all the other overheads, whether its buses are full or half empty. Its break-even analysis is therefore quite straightforward. When the total of fares paid on each run equals the overheads of the run, the bus company has reached break-even point.

Other costs that companies incur are called variable costs and only occur when a customer buys something. These are the cost of the ingredients on the plate in the restaurant or the cost of buying the pen to sell in the newsagent. The more you sell, the higher the variable costs, but since you're selling the items for more than you paid for them, you'll also see a higher contribution from the sales towards your fixed costs and subsequently your profits. People call it all sorts of things, but I find the word 'contribution' fits the bill best. When you have worked out the difference between what customers paid for your products and what you paid for them, you have the contribution; that is, the profit that revenue has made to fixed costs.

Here's the formula in equation form:

Revenues – direct costs = contribution – fixed costs = net profit

You will, I'm afraid, hear these terms and others to describe the same equation, but it's easy enough to work out what the words mean if you fully understand the concept.

It should be easy enough to know your fixed costs. Don't fool yourself, though; if some are slightly uncertain, take the higher end of the possibilities. It's crucial to start with an accurate estimate of these costs. If you guess too high that's better than going the other way; you can always adjust the estimate when you have real experience as the months go by. Don't forget to put something in for yourself – unless you can live on air.

The next bit is trickier. You have to put together an estimate of the contribution that you'll make when the customers start buying. This can also be straightforward if you're selling a small number of easily identifiable products – an art gallery, for example, knows what it paid for each picture and therefore the profit it will make if it sells it for the price on the tag.

But life is not always so easy. Let's start with a simple example to make the point. Suppose you were running a pub that sold only Guinness. From your supplier, you would know exactly how much each pint you sell has cost you.

I'm going to ignore VAT for the purposes of this exercise. Here's the equation where the selling pint of a price is £3 and you buy it in at £1. The contribution for each pint is £3 − £1 = £2. Your fixed costs are £1200 per week, so you need to sell 600 pints (1200 divided by 2) to cover the fixed costs. So 600 pints is your break-even point.

That way it's dead easy; but this Guinness-only scenario is unlikely to be the case because you'll sell all sorts of other drinks too. But if you stick with drinks only, you should be able to estimate the average cost of all the drinks you sell. You can use that figure for planning purposes and adjust it with experience. For example, if your average drinks price for the whole range is £3.50, the average variable cost is £1.50 and your fixed costs have risen to £1600 per week, then you need to divide 1600 by 2 (3.50 − 1.50) to find out the number of drinks you have to sell – 800 with sales revenue of £2800.

But, of course, you sell food as well and the margin on food ingredients is very different from those on drinks. Again, you have to make an estimate. Using your common sense, you'll work out a reasonable way of doing it. Perhaps you estimate the ratio of drinks to food that customers will consume. Say at lunchtime someone who spends £6 on food is likely to spend £5 on two drinks. In the evening many people will only drink, but a customer who spends £15 on food may well spend £12 on drinks. And so on.

However you do it, you now have an estimate of the contribution that sales make to fixed costs and profits. Say your best estimate is an overall contribution of 50%, because on average you sell the products for double the price you paid for them. And let's say your monthly fixed costs are £6000. At what point does the contribution from sales equal the total of your fixed costs? That's your break-even point.

Try to get your hands on the stock takes of some other pubs. This will show you the likely product mix. The mix varies quite a lot from pub to pub. Pubs with sport will have a much higher percentage of beer, while a club will lean towards spirits.

So, take this example in equation form:

Sales	12,000
Variable costs	6,000
Gross profit	6,000
Fixed costs	6,000
Profit	0

If you do this on a spreadsheet you can play with it to your heart's content. You can try halving the sales and see how bad the situation could become. You could have another look at your fixed costs and see if there are any economies there, and so on.

WHAT I LEARNT NOT TO DO

It's bound to come up at some point, so I'll mention it here. Not everyone is trustworthy, so don't regard anyone as being 100% honest until they've really proved it. If your business is a fast-moving consumer goods business like a bar, you are exposed to the risk of staff stealing from you. In one of our early businesses, we had a stock shortage of no less than £29,000 in the first summer of trading. Our 'mates' behind the bar had been ripping us off big time. My experience is that the people who are the friendliest are often the ones who are stitching you up. By all means get to know your staff and socialize with them because, in many cases, people who know you well are less likely to steal from you; but you should *never* let your guard down completely.

Using break-even analysis for budgeting

If you've done the break-even exercise, you'll find it useful in many ways. First of all, it gives you your budget. This is the estimate of the first year's figures and is essential for your bank manager if you're borrowing money, or your shareholders if you're trying to attract capital from investors.

When you add in the one-off costs of fitting out, you can see how long it takes to recover that money as well. This has an impact on the decisions you make about how much to spend. If, for example, your break-even analysis shows that you won't recover the fitting-out costs for a long time, you may decide to go for something a bit cheaper.

Once you've covered your fixed costs, all additional contribution goes straight to the bottom line. Or does it? Basically that statement is true; but lots of people get caught out by factors that occur as the business grows and that perhaps they haven't taken into account. If, as a result of rising sales, your shop needs another shop assistant, this will cause a sudden rise in fixed costs. And you can't hire a third of a person, so sales will have to increase further to break even, until the increase in profits has covered the costs of employing a new person. Make sure that you make provision in your plan for those times when the fixed costs will take such a leap.

Here's an example of a business facing a sudden increase in fixed costs. Two partners in a restaurant started out with one running the restaurant and the other staying in her job. She was understandably anxious to leave her job and get on with creating the restaurant they dreamt of running. She resigned just before the business had achieved break even. This basically added £2,500 a month to their overheads and further delayed break even. I think that this was a bit risky, and that they might have been better to wait a while until the business could absorb the extra overhead and still break even.

In a pub, the core business is selling drinks. If you can cover your fixed costs from the contribution of the drinks side, then any contribution from food goes directly to the bottom line. This is pretty well true and I find the same goes for any core business. For example, you can reverse this if you're running a restaurant whose core attraction is food. Cover your fixed costs with the food, and the contribution from drinks goes straight into your pocket.

Final point – make sure that you do this planning work before you sign any contracts for leases or anything. I know of a business whose owners disobeyed this rule and signed up for their premises before they knew their break-even point. It was a boat business and when they finally did the analysis, they found that they needed to spend £400 per day on fuel. Then they had to let people on and off the boat at a place where someone else had built a jetty, so they incurred docking fees of £150 per day. Now add in staff and other running costs and suddenly the break-even point was 200 passengers per day. This was a massively challenging target and they realized that they were unlikely to hit it; but they'd signed up for the boat. Whether they liked the break-even point or not, they were stuffed into going ahead with buying the boat and starting a business that looked very dodgy from day one. It's a bit optimistic to make any commitments before you've done the numbers; it looks too much like emotion getting in the way of sound business common sense. A lot of this comes down to experience – so make sure that you know your business area before you start. Remember that the proverbial fool is soon separated from their cash.

So, you know your estimated fitting-out costs, your running costs, your product profit margins and your break-even point. Is your idea financially viable? Can you in the end get enough customers to spend the amount of money necessary to break even and, if so, how long do you think it will take? Can you see further growth from that point to start to make a really substantial profit? Well done: you now have a rough financial plan.

5   THE DECISION TO LEASE PREMISES OR BUY THEM

You have to make an early decision on buying or leasing your premises. The argument is mainly a financial one. But make sure that it's the right decision for the long term by only tying up the capital that's right for the situation.

The implications of owning assets

If you decide to lease, the impact on your profits and cash flow is the monthly or quarterly rent that will be reviewed at the intervals specified in the lease agreement. You've also got the upfront premium to pay where appropriate as a one-off cost. So it's straightforward to see the impact of the lease on your profit and loss account and cash flow. If you decide to buy the property, it becomes an asset with a value that can go either up or down. This is much less predictable than the leasing option, although premiums paid for leasing go up and down as well. Owning assets can complicate things quite a bit.

Now, once you've got fixed assets, such as a property, you may find it useful to check how successfully you're using them to make money. In some industries it is very relevant to look at a management ratio that measures this return on assets. It's a simple calculation to compare the value of the fixed assets used in a business to the profits that you're making out of them. This measure says to the owners of the business: 'What profits can you make out of the assets you own, and how much more will you earn if you buy more assets?' It's a measure that the stock market uses quite extensively, so it affects share prices and company values. It could be a measure that a potential buyer of your business will take into account. Since the price of property has plummeted, this ratio is much more likely to look healthy. As always there's a downside – the difficulty of getting mortgage money at a sensible cost – but if you can do it you can add the rise in the value of your property to the value of your business.

In terms of making your first million, it could be useful to measure the success of different outlets where they have widely differing values using the return-on-assets figure. Suppose you have an opportunity to buy premises in a prestigious high-street location. You will obviously take the expensive costs of the outlet into account through the profit and loss account, in that you will charge the interest on the high mortgage you had to take out to buy the property; but what about the capital you put in from the cash resources of the business? To make sure that you are getting as good a return on the new asset as you are from the others, use the return-on-assets ratio as a valid comparison.

In some large companies there are huge political battles, with many managers pleading their case to the powers that be that big, expensive assets – some really quite old – should be on the balance sheet of their profit centre rather than someone else's. This ignores the fact that they are going to be measured on how efficiently the business uses its assets. And the more assets you've got, the higher the return you would be required to make on them. This is another example where business managers look at their businesses quite differently from entrepreneurs. Entrepreneurs get no warm feeling if they own business assets; they're constantly thinking about profits so that they can spend their money on the assets that do interest them, the ones in their long driveways and lying berthed at Monte Carlo. Mind you, there's a lot to be said for not having landlords. In my experience they can be a right pain in the butt.

This points up why I quite often shy away from buying premises. I prefer to lease and use any extra cash I might have because of that decision to lease another outlet, and so on. It basically means that I can concentrate on the return on my investment rather than working on making the assets sweat to give me a better return on assets. So there is no intrinsic value in owning assets and you mustn't get carried away by thoughts of being even more independent an operator if you own things. Having said that, owning your own premises does carry some important benefits. You don't have rent reviews, so the cost of the premises only goes up and down with interest rates, and you don't have a landlord, some of whom are very, very unreasonable. Keep looking at the whole project in terms of the overall aim of making the first million as fast as you can.

Another thought on ownership is that the asset only remains an asset at the price you bought it for if you can sell it to someone who believes they can make money out of it. That is, if you've built up a property asset as a retail outlet of some sort and you can't make enough money out of it, you can only sell it to someone who thinks they can do better than you. I know it's negative thinking, but it's worth sparing a thought for what you could sell an asset for if the business doesn't fly. Indeed, if you've bought property, you may very well recoup a major part of your losses through any increase in the price of the asset when you sell it. But suppose your big idea was to buy an old steamer and convert it cleverly into a floating restaurant, offering moonlit cruises combined with haute cuisine in the Lake District; and suppose you got into the situation where it's breaking even but not making real money. You may find it very difficult to get the value of the steamer and the work done on it from a potential buyer. The argument is that if the current owners can't turn a profit out of such an extraordinary asset, who else can?

We can learn about business start-ups from the huge expansion of golf courses over the last decade or so in the south-east of England. They're constructed, because of their location, on relatively expensive land. In many cases the original owners were hamstrung by massive amounts of debt, had to sell membership at much lower rates in order to attract golfers from the competition, and so on. Many of them lost the battle and had to get out. What is the value of the asset? Certainly it is a lot less than they paid for it and spent on it. Venture capitalists bought the courses up at bargain prices and paid off some debt, which relieved the profit and cash-flow problem.

They then allowed time for the membership to grow until the point at which the business was about breaking even, or a little better. They then sold it on to the third owners, normally a company that owned several such courses and which, with the benefits of scale, was able to make it into a nice, profitable business. We can learn four lessons from this:

- The start-up is the most risky part of the company food chain and you've got to have a realistic, honest plan that shows that you can make a viable idea fly.
- Venture capitalists have no interest in the underlying business – they want to get in and out as quickly as possible.
- When you're planning your exit strategy, think about larger companies that, using economies of scale, could make your business even more profitable.
- When you've grown into a business with a bit of a track record and a good profit stream, look for expansion by buying start-ups at the struggling stage. You can sometimes get them for a lot less money than their value to you, particularly when property prices are low.

If you do want to make a decision based on detailed financial evaluation, however, here's how to do it. Assume for the moment that all other things are equal: you will sell the same amount of goods from the shop however you occupy it, owner or tenant. Now make a five-year cash-flow projection of the outgoings involved for each method. Get the insurance side right and the rates and all the other expenses. Now discount the cash flow for time and arrive at the net present value of the two methods and decide on the better of the two. If you don't know how to do this, get your accountant to show you and don't leave his or her office until you can do it. To be honest, I don't use this technique. It's much more a big company thing, but I've included it for completeness' sake. While most entrepreneurs take future plans on a fair amount of gut feel, it's interesting to note that, as their businesses get bigger, they all understand that money in their pocket now is worth more than the same amount in a few years' time.

At business school they teach you how to depreciate the value of assets over time using some pretty strict rules. But I don't really buy the benefit of this for normal day-to-day business decisions. If you take the value of assets into account when you're buying a business, you can make some pretty iffy decisions as opposed to taking a strict view of the business's profit record and whether you think this is going to be maintained or grow.

You see, the value of an asset is always one person's opinion. A way to remember that there can be a huge difference between what the figures say and what the physical reality is, comes in the shape of the old story of the jobbing builder who claimed to his bank manager, through his balance sheet, to have a fixed asset of a cement mixer and a stock of cement. In fact, when the bank manager visited the premises and looked around, he found that the cement mixer had hardened concrete in it. While the balance sheet was accurate, the truth was that neither the fixed asset nor the cement held in stock had any value at all.

I know that assets are sometimes involved in valuations, particularly if the assets are property; but it's always safer to value a business purely and simply by its ability to make profits. OK, that's probably enough about the theory of assets and their value to enable you to take the financial decision whether to lease or buy.

6 DRAWING UP A DETAILED BUSINESS PLAN

Whether you like it or not, you're going to have to present a case to a bank if you want to borrow money from it. Most banks ask you to fill in some standard forms. Here's what the forms include, and a few tips on presenting the best possible case.

The upside of the dreaded banking forms

Bank managers have heard it all before. Almost all businesspeople tell them that their particular business is different and that a banker shouldn't use the same parameters to judge their business as they do others. Bank managers therefore spend a lot of time convincing their new customers that, while to a certain extent it is true that all businesses do have different detailed characteristics, nevertheless no business can ignore the universal issues that any profit-making company has to take into account. No matter how difficult it is in, for example, a service company to calculate and monitor gross margin, the managers of the business must do it. Another truth that people sometimes plead to be different in their environments is the rule that everything in business is negotiable. No one – lawyer, accountant, financial adviser or supplier of anything – works in a vacuum, therefore everything is negotiable. You don't have to fill out the bank's forms if you've done your own cash flow, by the way. They'll be impressed that you've gone to that trouble before you were asked.

All this is to defend the generalized forms that banks make their potential business borrowers fill in before they'll consider their case. If the ideas in this section seem like reasonable preparation work, then I've made the point. I've used the headings and order of one of the major banks' start-up forms.

We should take them seriously for a number of reasons:

- You need to manage carefully your relationship with the bank, and this is their first taste of the new boy's or girl's professionalism.
- Whatever business you are going into, the great majority of the forms are completely relevant.

- Filling them in ensures that you've thought through the points they asked for and then converted them into a profit and loss account and cash-flow statement.
- They are comprehensive. If you've filled them all in apart from the bits that genuinely do not apply to your business, you can rest assured you have covered all the angles.
- They are the first and probably the last bit of free consultancy and subsequent discussion that the bank will give you. Don't take too much notice of bank managers, though. If they really knew about making money, they'd be doing it rather than sitting behind a desk talking to you.
- The forms are mainly there so that bank managers can tick the boxes and cover themselves should it all go wrong later. Make sure you've done your own cash flow and profit calculation exercises and that they're realistic.

Now, don't forget the point about negotiation. If you find it difficult to fill in one set of bank forms, then you may not relish the thought of doing two. And yet, that is what you've got to do if you're to get the best deal. You need to play one off against another. If, for some reason, one bank turns your case down, then go to a third and try again. Perhaps that way you can still get two offers to compare after all. You may also find, if the second bank has turned you down, that there's a flaw in your plan that you really do need to address.

Presenting a good business plan to your banker is highly important. It forms part of the 'contract' between you and the bank. The bank manager will use it, particularly the numbers part, to monitor your progress and spot things that are slipping early on. So don't make it so rosy that you are seen to come unstuck in the first six months. They'll never believe anything you say if that happens.

I would add one more significant point. The objective of the business plan is to get the money from the bank. It's not necessarily everything you have in your mind and there may be some bits in it that you've written down to please the potential lender. It's a selling document, nothing more and nothing less. If it's convincing, you get the money; if it's not, you don't. Bank managers worry about their jobs and have targets to make. Wow them with your professionalism and upbeat manner and you're halfway there. Everyone likes a winner, especially in hard times.

The forms themselves

Here are the questions you're going to have to answer.

What is your target market?

Think long and hard about who your customers will be. Paint a picture of the people themselves, and make sure you've talked to as many of them as you can. The more evidence you can give that the target market exists, the stronger this part of the plan will be. Now try to group them in some way. It may make sense to think about large and small customers, or ones who will travel for your type of service and those who only shop close to home. Only you can organize a sensible grouping. A sandwich shop might group its customers as:

1 Regulars
2 Passing trade
3 Offices and shops that order in advance

The point of this grouping is to identify later on in the process where greater opportunities lie and where better margins and profits can be found. This may mean that you start off looking for the business that's easiest to get, just to get some sales. But you may decide in the longer term that an emphasis on marketing and selling to another group will, once you've cracked into it, give you better profits or larger contracts.

Even at this stage there's a point to dreaming a bit. If you made some alterations to the product or service, could you reach another type of customer? Write the options down; once a great idea is documented it can never be lost. Remember while you're at this planning stage that dreams are about the unknown as well as the known. Indeed, it is bound to be true that following your dreams will take you in unexpected directions.

Do you really understand your customers and what they want?

Customers always trade product or service features against the price they are prepared to pay. They also look for how well your business provides customer satisfaction and what sort of relationship they can build with your people. To build long-term customer loyalty you need to understand their buying criteria – what questions will they use to compare you with your competitors? To understand this thoroughly, you have to talk to as many customers or potential customers as you can. What are they looking for? How do they make their decisions to buy?

Now you need to assess what your customers would say was their view of the ideal offering in each of the following four areas: product, process, people and price. Again, you can ask them for their opinion of what would be best for them by, for example, accosting likely people in the street with a clipboard. The points they make are their buying criteria and will fit into one of the four factors mentioned above. Customers will tell you what they ideally want from you, if you ask the right questions. You may not be able to achieve the ideal the customer is searching for but, if you know what it is, you should be able to come close.

Not all the criteria will have the same importance to a customer, so the final step in this technique is to put a priority against each one. When you've finished defining buying criteria and the customer's ideal, think about their relative importance on a scale of 1–10.

When it comes to making decisions about what your offering is going to be, you do not want to work hard on issues that customers think are less significant, if it means putting less effort into issues that they believe to be vital. These priorities will therefore have an impact on product, process, people and price decisions later in the planning process. Chart the result of this work on a matrix.

Customer value statement

Criteria group	Criteria	Customer ideal	Priority
Product or service What you supply to your customer	e.g. quality, or reliability	e.g. as good as a London restaurant	8
Process How you deal with your customer	e.g. prompt service	order taken within three minutes of going in	3
People The quality of the people who deal with the customer	e.g. good product advice on matters like wine	e.g. makes recommendations with a reason for the choice	5
Price The cost of the product or service to the customer	e.g. competitive	e.g. no higher than similar local quality	7

When you fill out the bank forms that cover this area of meeting customer needs and having unique competitive reasons for them to come to you rather than anywhere else, this matrix is a great demonstration of your professionalism in this key area. Tack it on at the back of the forms.

Who are your competitors?

If you have a lot of competitors, you may have to choose a few key ones to analyse. There are many sources of competitive information. You should obtain your competitors' brochures and promotional material to understand what they believe are their strengths and how they present themselves to customers. Relevant trade journals have comparisons of products and reviews of suppliers. Your customers and prospects are a great source of competitive knowledge, as are people who join your organization from a competitor. Now relate this information to your customers by making a chart of your competitors' ability to meet the decision criteria in your customer value matrix. You should note down in what areas they appear to be nearer to the customers' ideal than you are.

This may not be relevant for all businesses, but it's worth a thought: most organizations see their current competitors as providers of similar products or services. In fact this is not the case. There's often another way of doing things. If, for example, you intend to run a helicopter service carrying business people out to remote islands, a current competitor may be another contractor offering to run the same route. It's possible that future competitors may be videoconferencing companies which would render the journey unnecessary. Think about what your customer requires and what other ways they could meet their needs apart from using your types of products and services. Think widely about competitive possibilities, because it's certain that there are other organizations thinking widely about their prospects in your chosen markets.

The market does not stand still and neither do your competitors. What a customer found interesting and satisfying for even a long time in the past will not last for ever. Whole organizations have, in the past, been caught out because a product feature introduced by a competitor has become desirable and even fashionable. You have to be ready for such a change, or to react quickly if you did not anticipate the event. In the end you're going to have to explain to customers and prospects why they should prefer your offering to others. So work it out now, and keep working at it until you've convinced yourself.

Who are the key people in your organization?

If you are going to build a business you will almost certainly have to attract some key people who will help you go for the dream. Make sure that you've agreed their role and their responsibilities. Check that their experience is entirely relevant to that role and examine their network. People who join you will bring their own contacts and networks that will help you in expanding sales. Write those down along with their qualifications and skills. If you do this for everyone, including yourself, you will have a concise record of the starting point of the skills in the business. This offers good sales points for the banker, because it makes you look professional and meticulous.

Is your plan to reach your market realistic?

At some point, depending on the business you're in, you're going to have to spend money on promotions, advertising mailshots and other types of marketing. Take the fliers out to people in the street and try to discuss it with them. Ask little groups walking past your premises to come in and look at what you're thinking of doing. Their feedback will help to answer this question convincingly. You can put together focus groups as well – they give you good information and it's free.

At this planning stage, look at what your competitors do in terms of advertising and assess what it would cost to match them. Then decide whether that's a good idea in your first year before adding it to your estimated profit and loss account.

In my experience, getting in to see someone gives the best chance of making a sale. It is a good idea to be wary of the company catch-all brochure. Selling is about understanding what your potential customers want and need, and there's a limit to how well you can do that with a brochure that you're going to send out to a lot of people. Too much information is a turn-off. Stick to a clear, obvious message that shouts from the page. If it's relevant to your business and you use mailshots, always follow up by telephone to as many of these as you can. Ask to go and see people for ten minutes to get their feedback to the mailshot itself. This approach is a good sieve. If the person agrees to see you, you're making progress; if they don't, then their 'I'll think about it' or 'Just send me the company brochure' is simply a polite way of ending the telephone call. It is, of course, a faith position; but I don't really believe in company brochures that cover everything you do – they are no substitute for material that sells a particular item to a particular customer.

A woman setting up a service for looking after and entertaining children had to speak to a lot of mothers to get her first sessions filled up. To begin with, she started the conversation by explaining what the service was going to be and how it was going to grow. She got a much better hit rate when she started all the conversations by asking detailed questions about the mother's situation and requirements. We keep coming back to it – don't bang on about your products, listen to what your customers want.

Is your price right?

You are by now well aware of the profit margins available in your business. Work out a pricing policy that makes the best of these and is at the same time competitive. Look at how your customers expect to pay. If you're going to have account customers, what credit terms will they want? What can you offer that will be a trade-off for getting shorter payment terms than usual? Remember, a start-up has the least flexibility in waiting for money to come in – it's the most strapped for cash. So if that's your position, be innovative in looking for reasons you should be paid early and, at best, upfront.

Now, look at the business processes that you will need to have in place to chase your debtors and make them pay as near to the agreed date as you can. Who will do this chasing?

Who's going to do the selling and what's the bonus scheme?

Finally, think about the salespeople you're going to employ. These people are key to your early success if you need more than just yourself to do the selling. Even if the actual job is waiting tables, the real role is selling.

I think that, initially at least, you should avoid using share options as a way of attracting and motivating salespeople unless it's absolutely necessary. Under virtually no circumstances would I do this. It's your business, so don't give it away. If you accept this advice, you're almost certainly going to need to have some other sort of bonus scheme to get your salespeople selling what you want them to. This is crucial.

It can be tricky if you're in a business that has to negotiate discounts. If you make the bonus scheme a straight percentage of sales, you could have problems with the price at which sales are made. Most salespeople will happily make a sale by throwing in a 10% discount – for instance, selling something for £90 rather than working harder for the full price of £100. After all, giving things away is much easier than selling them. You'll have to explain to them that by giving away 10% of the selling price they are actually giving away 33% of the profit – or even more. Work it out if you don't believe me. Here's an example of a product with a low gross margin to illustrate the point.

	At full price	Discounted
Sale	100	100
Discount price by 10%	0	90
Cost of sale	60	60
Overheads	25	25
Profit	15	5

The selling price may only have gone down by 10%, but the net profit has dropped by 66%.

I have seen owners of businesses do very well by giving salespeople incentives to achieve the gross margin – sales price minus the cost of the product or service sold – rather than the actual sales price. That way the motivation is to sell at list price. This may be a more expensive sales bonus scheme, but it could easily earn its costs. If there's no share option to offer the people who are responsible for growing your business, then they're going to be expensive. As usual, it's a trade-off, but there is no point in being in business if you do not sell your products and services at a healthy price – so get it right.

Where are your premises?

The bank will want to know quite a lot about the terms and conditions of your premises if you're going to have them. You need to consider the following:

- What are the terms?
- If it is a renewable lease, how much will it be to renew it?
- If it is rented, when is the next rent review?
- What are the business rates?
- What insurance will you need?
- How long will this space last, and would it be better to allow a bit more for expansion?

How you fit out your premises is also vital, so be prepared to explain that. Make sure that there's complete consistency between the plan for the premises and your target market. The banker will want to be in no doubt that your premises will be attractive to the type of person you've described at the beginning of this banking forms process. They will also want to check that you've got the appropriate planning consents.

What are the equipment and other start-up costs?

'Premises' is a cost item that people choose because of their location rather than anything else, and that tends to dictate the ballpark price the lessor will charge. You have much more control over the price of fitting out. The main tip here is not to get a design and a price to build premises that indulge your own tastes – by doing so you'll almost certainly pay more than is necessary. Choose a design that you think will attract your customers and then purchase it at the cheapest possible price.

Investing in the latest technology and making full use of it can sometimes be worth it in the end, but beware: I've seen lots of businesses that have been talked into buying technology they didn't really need. Generally speaking, I prefer to keep things simple and stay as low tech as possible. Today's expensive technology will cost half as much in a couple of years and will have been superseded by something flashier. Try doing a cost–benefit analysis on it. Look at the alternative and try to cost that as well. If buying a piece of accounting software means that you or your spouse can do the bookkeeping, think of the saving that will make in your accountant's fees. The more you can do yourself in terms of printing plans in colour, doing your own copying and having your own website, the more control you have over your business and the lower are your running costs. It's the fixed costs that can be a problem when sales are poor in a tough environment or when you are starting up. Aim for investment now in areas that keep those running costs to a minimum.

Having said that, don't skimp on hiring a techie to design your website if you're not competent to do a professional job yourself. It's the only view most of the world has of you; so don't make it look amateurish for the sake of £500.

Take into consideration the following questions when considering technology purchases:

- How will you buy it?
- How long will it last? (Remember, £500 spent today on computers will almost certainly require another £500 in 12–18 months.)

- What are the running costs? Cheap printers cost a fortune in toner.
- Will you need training expenses to be able to make use of it?

Finish this exercise and you have done the difficult part of the planning process. Now you've got to do the numbers. You need a profit and loss account and a cash-flow statement. The cash flow is the document you need to keep up to date, so here are some pointers about how to do that.

Producing a good cash-flow statement depends on four things, one of which should be easy, the second gets easier with time, the third takes up much more time than you could possibly imagine and the fourth is a bastard.

1 An accurate estimate of your fixed costs: When you did your documentation for the bank you will have filled out the expenses and wages sheet that identifies your fixed costs. As you add to them, keep this number up to date. Remember, this is a cash flow so you do not include any depreciation that comes off your monthly profit and loss account. If you are depreciating fixed assets such as computer equipment, for example, the cash implication will be under capital expenditure on the week you buy the equipment, or in fixed costs as loan repayments if that is how you financed it. Its value, remember, is an opinion; we are only interested in the reality.

2 Variable costs are those costs that only occur when you make products or deliver services. The cash flow will include the details of the money spent on production as it occurs. If you sell the services of consultants but they are on your books, you should include them in fixed costs – you have to pay for them whether they are working

or not. If you employ casual labour only when you have work for them, you will have to become good at estimating your profit margin as you sell them on. So a building contractor will take a view on the percentage of sales that comes through as variable costs. It will not be very accurate, but there will be sufficient compensating errors if you work on the conservative side to ensure a reasonably true picture. Think hard about your variable costs and improve your ability to estimate them and understand the timing of payments. Always add a contingency to err on the side of caution. Refits, for example, always cost more than you think.

3 The third element of all this concerns your skills in getting your bills paid. Don't underestimate how much time needs to be allocated to it, and spend money on a resource to do it for you if it is taking up too much of your time.

4 And finally the bastard. The top line of a cash flow is the sales forecast – the most difficult estimate of them all. Not only do you have to guess how many units you will sell, you also have to estimate when the orders and deliveries will happen. Add to this the problem that you might not get all the orders you bid for because you will lose some to the competition. You know you will lose some, but which ones?

On the next two pages is an example of a fairly rough-and-ready cash flow for a contractor with various levels of gross margin. It was prepared by an expert contractor rather than an accountant, who might find it a bit inelegant, but it does the job. Management can see what needs to be done to ensure a satisfactory cash position.

Review this on at least a monthly basis. Do it weekly if you are managing a difficult situation. The trick is to generate one that reflects your business very well and needs little work to update it. Doing it without a spreadsheet on a computer is truly doing it the hard way.

Income from current debtors @ 6 Dec	Total	Dec	Jan	Feb	Mar	April	May	June	July	Item	Notes
Customer 1	30000	30000								1	The doubtful payer is not shown
Customer 2	3300	3300									
Customer 3	11500	6000	5500							2	Uninvoiced retentions of £25K not shown, part of which will be incoming over the period shown
Customer 4	14000	7000	7000								
Customer 5	5500	1500	4000								
Insurance claim	3000			3000						3	Receipts from current debtors are agreed payment dates
Others	2000	1000	1000							4	Sales receipts assumed to take: 50% 60 days. 50% 30days
Debtor income	69300	48800	17500	**3000**							

Expected sales	Value	Dec.	Jan	Feb	Mar	April	May	June	July	5	Overheads assessed and include
Customer 6	132000		13000	44000	30000	45000					staff
Others	31000	31000	0	0	0	0	0	**0**		6	Creditors are assumed to be stretched upto 60 days
Total sales	163000	31000	13000	44000	30000	45000	**0**				
Sales receipts	Debtors	48800	17500	3000							7	Figures shown do not include the effect of VAT
From sales	30 days		15500	6500	22000	15000	22500	0			
From sales	60 days			15500	6500	22000	15000	22500	0		
Total receipts	232300	48800	33000	25000	28500	37000	37500	22500	**0**		
Fixed costs		11000	11000	11000	11000	11000	11000	11000	11000		
Cost of sales											
Customer 6 @ 20% mark up					10833	36667	25000	37500		8	
					0	0	0	0	0		
Other @ 20% mark up			20000	25833	0	0	0	0	0		
Total outgoing		11000	31000	36833	21833	47667	36000	48500	**11000**		
Cash flow balance		Dec	Jan	Feb	Mar	April	May	June	July		
Bank		0									
Add sales receipts		48800	33000	25000	28500	37000	37500	22500	0		
Reduce by outgoing costs		11000	31000	36833	21833	47667	36000	48500	11000		
Cash position		37800	2000	-11833	6666.7	-10667	1500	-26000	**-11000**		
Cumulative		37800	39800	27967	34633	23967	25467	-533.3	**-11533**		
						Balance @ end of July			-11533		

7 THE FORMAL DOCUMENTATION OF STAFF APPRAISAL

The key to managing the managers in your business is that they understand entirely what you expect them to achieve. While you will talk to them frequently on a continuous basis about how well they are performing, you do need to sit down with them from time to time and formally evaluate their performance. It's an opportunity for you to show your appreciation and write it down. It's also an opportunity for them to say how they feel. Finally, it's an opportunity to work out how they could make a bigger contribution to the business and achieve their aims of furthering their career.

This means that you need three documents:

- Job description.
- Appraisal.
- Personal development plan. (This last one is a bit picky and I have never found the time to use them.)

The job description is the agreement between you and the manager of their objectives and key tasks. Once you have completed it, there should be no room for disputes about what they are meant to do. My method is to jot down my own notes about the job and then get them to flesh it out into the actual objectives.

A good job description gives you a number of benefits. It ensures that there are no misunderstandings; it gives you something to give to an agency if you are looking for new people; and it gives you the ability to agree with the person how the role is changing as the business itself changes.

The final benefit is that it makes the holding of an annual appraisal relatively straightforward. The two of you are just agreeing to what extent the manager has fulfilled their role. Then you can talk about their strengths and weaknesses in order to find the way ahead. Always talk about their strengths first, but don't shirk from discussing the weaknesses.

A good appraisal makes it easier to agree someone's personal development plan. Perhaps they need some training; perhaps they could gain some experience in a secondment, either into another job in another part of the organization or in a staff job helping you to push the business forward. In any case, people are much happier if they see you taking their career seriously as well as their performance in the current job.

In the end, most entrepreneurs take a less formal approach than this. When business is tough, how much time do you have for proper human resources processes? You're more engaged in getting money off from your suppliers. You simply tell people what you expect. Some shine, and you fire the others.

SUGGESTION BOX

If you're still with a big organization, use the huge amount of financial knowledge it holds by talking to a friendly financial controller. Once again, most people are happy to display their knowledge of a subject to a beginner, so it should be easy enough. If you can't tell them that it's for your own planning purposes, tell them it's for your partner or a mate or whatever. Ask them for advice on finding small business software that you could study. Go online to Companies House and buy the profit and loss account and balance sheet of a small retailer. It'll cost you a few pounds and it could just give you a shortcut to the knowledge you need. But be very wary of these accounts – they can be misleading, and you may need an accountant to have a quick look to see that you're interpreting them correctly. The point is, don't leave it until after you've left to set up the business: you'll have more than enough to do with everything else than doing your financial homework.

INDEX